JACKIE SHAW'S

Learn to Paint

FRUITS & VEGETABLES

A Step-by-Step Approach to Beautiful Results

DESIGN ORIGINALS

an Imprint of Fox Chapel Publishing

www.d-originals.com

To my husband, Lynn, who truly is "the wind beneath my wings."

ACKNOWLEDGMENTS

Part of the joy of doing a book like this is the opportunity it affords to meet new people while pursuing friends' leads. For this, we are grateful to Betty and Joe Frushour, Harold Stottlemyer, Gary Hoffman, Elsa Hoffman, and Priscilla Harsh.

A large measure of joy results from having to stretch and grow and watching as family also stretches to accommodate an increasingly frenetic schedule and mushrooming needs. This book is as much my husband Lynn's as it is mine. It would have been impossible without his help organizing and managing the computer files; finding things I misfiled (or failed to save) in that wondrous, exasperating electronic vacuum; prodding the computer back into service every time it called "time out!"; keeping track of the hundreds of photographs and illustrations; keying every image and bit of text so they would appear in the proper places in the book; and particularly for loving and appreciating me through it all. Special thanks go also to my mother, Grace Waters Bisese, and to our youngest daughter, Jen Reese, for helping with the manuscript; and to our two other daughters Kathy Graham and Laura Duvall; all three sons-in-law, Andy, John, and David; and grandchildren Savanah, Jimmy, Colton, Madison, Tommy, and Elena, for patiently enduring us while we focused single-mindedly on this book.

An enormous debt of gratitude goes to Mindie Conway who stepped in to relieve my worry and tend all my cherished gardens while I had to be content with the images from them on my computer screen.

For their generosity in providing unlimited access to their orchards, great appreciation goes to Clopper's Orchards in Smithsburg, Maryland, and to Margie and Lawrence Johnson in Valley Center, California.

For sharing and caring and patiently waiting for us to return to a normal life, special thanks to Jody and Nicholas Long and Heidi and Steve Lippman.

And of course, had it not been for all my wonderful students throughout the United States and abroad on whom I practiced and developed techniques, whose needs made me stretch, and whose sharing helped me grow, I would not have been able to do such a book. Special thanks to them all, and to the following magazines in which some of these lessons or variations first appeared: *Decorative Artist's Workbook, Tole World*, and *Quick and Easy Painting*.

ACQUISITION EDITOR: Alan Giagnocavo
DEVELOPMENTAL EDITOR: Margaret Riley
EDITOR: Katie Weeber

ISBN 978-1-4972-0010-4

Library of Congress Cataloging-in-Publication Data

Names: Shaw, Jackie, author.
Title: Jackie Shaw's learn to paint fruits & vegetables / Jackie Shaw.
Description: East Petersburg : New Design Originals Corporation, 2016. |
  Includes index.
Identifiers: LCCN 2015030247 | ISBN 9781497200104
Subjects: LCSH: Fruit in art. | Vegetables in art. | Painting--Technique.
Classification: LCC ND1400 .S53 2016 | DDC 745.7/23--dc23
LC record available at http://lccn.loc.gov/2015030247

Printed in Singapore
First printing

Every child is an artist. The problem is how
to remain an artist once he grows up.
—*Pablo Picasso*

INTRODUCTION

Capturing images, impressions, and emotions that stir us, and expressing them in paint, is one of life's great creative adventures. It gives us the opportunity for self-exploration, as well as creative self-expression. The creative process is an innate part of our being and allows us to indulge the "child" in us. Unfortunately, for many that innate creativity is submerged under fears and insecurities. If we worry about how our art or creativity will be perceived or judged by others, we paint with timidity and fear rather than with the free, exploring spirit we had as children.

Before we learned that we had to color neatly within the lines of the coloring book, and that dogs were not green, and walls were not for drawing on, we were all very creative. If you believe you are no longer creative, you need to know that you can be again; but you must regain your child-like daring and independence. You must be willing to experiment and to attempt the somewhat absurd at times, and to be flexible, nonconforming, and curious. You must redevelop your courage and self-confidence and, above all, be willing to risk failure in order to attain success. Before you learned to walk, you fell down a lot; but you grew stronger and more resolute in the process.

Be bold. Accept that you will paint some failures along the way, but try to learn from them. We learn more from our frustrating mistakes than from our easy successes. Be positive and expect to succeed. If you continually tell yourself, "I can't do this," you'll soon convince yourself, thus paving the way for failure. Think "I can," and you will!

CONTENTS

Getting Started

To get started, you'll need only a few basic brushes and paints. For the other supplies, you can "make do" with common household items to keep your initial expenses down. You don't even have to be able to draw, because I'll tell you several ways you can transfer patterns onto your surface. You may need to return to this chapter frequently in the beginning if the brush techniques discussed are new to you. So mark its location with a tab or ribbon for quick reference.

You've taken the first step on your painting adventure by picking up this book. Now let's get you started collecting supplies and learning how to use them.

Basic Supplies

You can get started on your lifetime of creative self-expression with just a small investment. Your most important tools are brushes and paints, of which there is a wide range of price and quality. Pamper yourself with the best quality you can afford. Your brushes, if well cared for, will last a long time. And quality paints (with lots of pigment) will help you achieve the results you seek, and are a joy to work with. Inferior products will undermine both your efforts and your confidence.

While it is handy to have an assortment of brush sizes, you can get by substituting the basic brushes listed below for other brushes and sizes suggested in the lessons. Mixing paints is a lot of trial and error to achieve a specific color. Don't panic—just mix and create.

PAINTS: DECOART AMERICANA ACRYLICS

Substitute your preferred paint brand and colors as desired. See page 8.
- Primary Red
- Primary Blue
- Yellow Light
- Titanium (Snow) White
- Lamp (Ebony) Black
- Purchase additional paints when you're ready, concentrating first on additional primary colors.

BRUSHES: LOEW-CORNELL SYNTHETIC TAKLON BRUSHES

Substitute your preferred brush brand and sizes as desired. See page 10.
- Flats: Nos. 2, 6, and 10 (Series 7300)
- Round: No. 2 (Series 7040)
- Liner: No. 1 (Series JS)

MISCELLANEOUS

- Paint extender medium
- Pad of 9- by 12-inch Bristol board (art paper), watercolor paper (hot pressed), or poster board to paint on
- Tracing paper for copying patterns

HOUSEHOLD ITEMS

· Jar of water (for rinsing brushes)
· Bottle cap or jar lid (for holding water or painting medium on the palette)
· Paper towels (for blotting brushes)
· Foam or wax-coated paper plates, foam meat tray, or freezer paper (shiny side only) for palette to squeeze paint on, to mix paint, and to blend paint on
· Plastic knife (for mixing paints)
· Pencil or chalk (for sketching and making transfer paper)
· Dead ballpoint pen (for transferring patterns)
· Soap (such as Ivory) for cleaning brushes
· Alcohol, fingernail polish remover, or acetone (for cleaning badly neglected brushes)
· Cotton swabs (for lifting out damp paint)
· Hair dryer (handy for speeding up the drying of paints)
· Old toothbrush (for spattering water onto acrylics on the palette to keep them moist)

Supplies for Special Backgrounds

There are a number of specialty and household items that can be used to achieve interesting background effects. On page 47 I explain a number of faux finish techniques, which make use of these supplies.

· 1" foam brush
· 2" sponge/foam paint roller
· Chip brush: 1" (Series 2053, for streaking)
· Flat wash brushes: ½", ¾", 1" (Series 7550)
· Sponges (synthetic or natural)
· Plastic wrap
· Plastic mesh bag
· Weathered wood finishing product
· Woodgraining comb
· Chamois cloth

WISH LIST ITEMS

· Flat brushes: Nos. 4, 8, and 12 (Series 7300)
· Round brushes: Nos. 0 and 4 (Series 7040)
· Liner brushes: Nos. 2 and 10/0 (Series JS)
· Dagger brush: ¼" (Series 7800)
· Round brush: No. 8 (Series Fabric Dye)
· Brush tub (for rinsing brushes)
· Plastic palette storage cups (for holding water and medium)
· Trowel-type palette knife (for mixing paints)
· Disposable paper palette (on which to squeeze and mix paints)
· Chacopaper in blue and white, plus graphite paper in black or gray.
· Stylus (for transferring patterns)
· Brush cleaner for acrylic paints (for cleaning brushes)
· Spray mister (to keep acrylics moist)
· Purchased or homemade wet palette (to keep acrylics fresh longer; see page 8)

ABOUT PAINTS

The paints used throughout the step-by-step lessons in this book are acrylics in squeezable bottles. My chosen brand is DecoArt Americana Acrylics, but you can substitute any brand or colors you prefer. Do be aware that some brands have similar paint names but their colors differ greatly. Or, they may have similar colors but quite different names. You can find conversion charts from one company to another online. If you already have other paints (tube acrylics, watercolors, oils) you can use them, making adjustments to accommodate their different attributes. Tube acrylics, other than needing a little more thinning for the washes and floated colors, will work like the bottled acrylics. Watercolors, which are traditionally used by building up layers of thin washes, respond similarly to the way acrylics work in washes. The greatest difference with acrylics is the use of colored backgrounds and opaque, colored undercoats. Oil paints, because of their slow drying time, do not lend themselves as readily to the buildup of thin layers. However, this technique was inspired by the old masters and their use of glazes over light undercoats to create luminous "glowing-from-within" effects. It just took longer drying periods and the use of drying agents added to their paints. A fast-drying oil paint, Genesis, can be heat set to hasten the drying time, thus allowing it to be used much like acrylics.

Prolonging the "Open Time"

The beauty of acrylics is that they dry quickly on our paintings. The frustrating thing about acrylics is that they dry quickly on our palettes. You can delay the drying time by mixing in a painting medium (see below) or by keeping a spray mister handy to mist the puddles of paint on your palette. Otherwise, flick water onto the paint piles with a wet toothbrush. You can also keep the paints workable longer by using a wet palette—a plastic box containing a sponge to be soaked in water and special water-absorbent palette paper that wicks water up into the puddle of paint. Create a makeshift wet palette by dipping a folded paper towel in water and covering it with a piece of deli paper or butcher/freezer paper. Paints squeezed onto that paper "sandwich" will dry more slowly than those squeezed onto a regular disposable palette.

Using Painting Mediums

Painting mediums or paint extender mediums are designed to extend the "open," or "working," time of the paint, rendering it more flexible and easier to work with when using techniques that require slower drying paints, such as applying washes. Use a medium of your choice. Any one medium can be mixed with acrylic paint to prolong the drying time. The medium can be applied directly to the surface or over layers of dry paint, and paint can then be worked into it while it is still wet. Painting mediums can also be used to render the paints more translucent: The greater the proportion of medium to paint, the more translucent the paint will be. Once the paint/medium mixture starts to set up on your painting, or feels like it's beginning to drag, avoid stroking over it further. It will no longer react smoothly. To prevent reactivating paint layers that have had medium added to them, dry them thoroughly with a hair dryer before making additional paint applications. Otherwise, moisture may cause the previous paint layer to lift off. If the surface is cool to the touch, it is not dry.

Most extender mediums are approximately the thickness of bottled acrylic paint. Use them directly from the bottle or thin them with water if a finer application is desired. Mix a little into your puddle of paint, or pick some up on the edge of your brush along with a little paint and blend them together on the palette.

The heaviest painting mediums, when applied directly to the painting surface or mixed into the paints, will allow you to move the acrylic paint around much like working with oil paint. Thicker mediums give the acrylics more body and thus help hold the paint in piles, rather than thinning it down into puddles.

Creating Paint Mixtures

The lessons and worksheets are designed to make it as easy as possible to paint each subject, without having to worry about too many color mixtures, and whether or not you've mixed exactly the right color.

Note: When you know the color you're trying to create, it's best to start with the lighter or weaker color and add the darker or stronger one to it. Some colors are more intense or have more overpowering pigment than others. If you wanted to mix pink, for example, and did so by adding white to red, you might end up with enough mixture to paint a room in your house before you achieved the light pink tint you wanted. Instead, add red to white, mixing in small increments at a time.

Surfaces to Paint On

One of the joys of working with acrylic paints is the ease with which they can be used for painting on a variety of surfaces. In this book, I have focused on the painting of subject matter and have worked primarily on assorted artists' papers. A block of inexpensive watercolor paper or a pad of Bristol board will serve sufficiently for practicing the lessons, although more expensive watercolor paper will yield happier results.

Matching Paint

When mixing paints, compare them to the area to be painted using the step-by-step worksheet for comparison. Lighten or darken as needed but most importantly mix colors that are pleasing to you.

ABOUT BRUSHES

Side/corner/edge

Chisel edge

Hairs —

— Heel

Metal ferrule —

Crimp —

Handle —

Take a minute to learn the names of the parts of a brush. They will be referred to throughout this book.

The Loew-Cornell series of brushes I recommend are composed of synthetic Taklon filaments, ideal for use with acrylic paints. They do not get easily waterlogged and limp as lesser quality brushes often do. In fact, they are quite resilient and snap back to their original shape after stroking with them. The flat brushes are evenly formed with sharp chisel edges, which are vital for painting careful details. Likewise, the round brushes form fine points, with no stray or uneven hairs to spoil your painted effects. The handles of the brushes are held snugly in their metal ferrules—a wobbly brush is no fun to paint with! These moderately priced brushes will serve you well if you treat them with the care they deserve. I clearly love working with these brushes, but as with any of the materials in this book, feel free to substitute the brushes listed with those of your preferred brand or size. If you are substituting brushes, look for the features described to help in your search.

Getting to Know Your Brushes

Your brushes can last a very long time, or become practically useless after your first painting session (that should get your attention!). Let's make sure yours last and remain in excellent condition, because it's difficult—to nearly impossible—to do great work with poor brushes.

Before using your brushes the first time, take a few minutes to familiarize yourself with them in their new condition. It will make it easier for you to keep them like new. First, remove the factory applied sizing that stiffens the hairs and protects them in shipment. Dip the hairs in water and squeeze them gently between your thumb and forefinger to loosen the sizing. Rinse the brush well, then dry it by stroking it on both sides on a soft cloth or paper towel. Notice how the bottom edge of the hairs forms a sharp, chisel edge. The hairs lie straight and tight together and have no outward curl. This tight grouping of the hairs makes managing paint easy. Curly hairs cause problems. A good quality, new brush should be resilient, with hairs that snap back quickly to their original shape after use, and no stray hairs. A waterlogged brush, or an inferior quality brush will have limp, unresponsive, uneven hairs.

Next, notice the smooth transition from the metal ferrule to the hairs. Slide your thumb and forefinger along the ferrule and off onto the hairs. Do this several times. Memorize the smooth feel of the transition. You don't notice any lumpy formation at the junction of the ferrule and the hairs. If paint is not meticulously cleaned from your brushes each time you use them, and even *while* you're using them, it will dry in the hairs at the base of the ferrule. Over time, a thick, hard knot will form, causing the hairs to splay out and open a sort of tunnel when looked at from the hair end of the brush. The hairs may also separate like teeth on a comb.

With splayed hairs, it is impossible to get a sharp chisel edge on the brush, making it hard to control where the paint is going to go.

The handle of your new brush fits snugly in its ferrule, held in place by the crimp; and with its highly lacquered finish it is a pleasure to hold. A brush left standing in water, which covers the ferrule and part of the wood handle, will soon loosen, a result of subsequent soaking and drying out. It's hard to control a wobbly handled brush. The swelling and shrinking of the wood will also cause the lacquer to crack and peel, making an unpleasant feeling handle. Left standing too long in water, the hairs of the brush will bend. And as unlikely as it sounds, acrylic paint will harden in the hairs even though they're submerged.

That's the bad news. The good news is you can prevent the premature demise of your brushes with attentive care.

Cleaning Your Brushes

Clean your brushes thoroughly at the end of each painting session. If you're working long or hard with the brushes, take a break and give them a good cleaning during the session. Don't leave them standing or dangling in water. They will become water logged and limp, and the acrylic paints will begin to set, even in the wet hairs. If you know your brushes are expensive, all the more reason to keep them cleaned.

1. Rinse out as much paint as possible, then stroke the hairs of the brush on a wet bar of soap, taking as much soap into them as possible. Or dip them in brush cleaner for acrylic paints. Do not scrub the hairs into the bar of soap or in the palm of your hand to load them with soap or cleaner. The scrubbing motion weakens and wears the hairs, causing them to break and curl.

2. With soap in the brush hairs, pinch the hairs between your thumb and forefinger, squeezing the soap up toward the ferrule. Wiggle the brush gently to work the soap amongst the hairs. Do not bend the hairs sharply against the ferrule.
3. Rinse well, then repeat steps 1 and 2 until every trace of color is gone. If any color remains to tint the soap, that means there is still paint in your brush. Tiny amounts left behind after each cleaning soon mount up to a big knot. So keep working.
4. When you're convinced no paint remains in the brush, rinse it well, then stroke it on the clean bar of soap once more. Leaving the soap in the brush, shape the hairs as they were when you first bought the brush: flat brushes to a smooth chisel edge; round brushes and liner brushes to a fine point.
5. Lay the brushes flat to dry. (If you stand them on their ends in a container before they are completely dry, some of the moisture that remains in the hairs and ferrule can drain down to the wood handle.) Place on a paper towel to dry. If you instantly see a tint of color on the paper towel, clean your brush again. Be sure your bristles are not leaning against another brush or your bristles will not dry into their original shape. Once they are dry, it's safe to store them in a jar (hairs up) or in a box or other container. The soap in the hairs will dry stiff to protect them and help them retain their like-new shape. Before using the brushes again, simply rinse them well.

(Whoops!) Repairing the Damage

What do you do if you accidently let paint dry in a brush or store it upside down? Accidents do happen. Distractions undermine our best intentions, and a paint-filled brush gets set aside and forgotten. Even though the paint has dried and the hairs are stiff as peanut brittle, don't throw the brush away.

Removing Hardened Paint

Soak the hairs in alcohol, acetone, or nail polish remover containing acetone. Remember to do this in a well-ventilated room. Take precautions to keep the fluid off the handle or it will dissolve the lacquer into a sticky mess.

Two ways to soak a damaged brush.

Do this:

Stroke your brush gently to load with soap.

Don't do this:

Do not scrub the hairs in a circular motion!

Squeeze the soap gently up toward the ferrule.

A jar lid or a saucer with a rim makes a good soaking dish. You can use a clothespin or two to elevate the brush at an angle into a saucer or lid. Stand the clothespin on its two "legs," letting the brush be the third "leg" of a tripod. Just be sure that the weight of the brush does not bend the hairs. Or, suspend the brush in a jar, so the hairs do not rest on the bottom, by using spring type clothespins to hold the handle. Cover the container with foil or plastic wrap if you can do so without including the brush handle. Concentrated fumes can also soften the lacquer.

After the dried paint has loosened, clean the brush as described before. The solvent soak is a harsh measure, so don't use it as a part of your regular cleaning routine. And as harsh as it is, it will not undo the tunnel or the split-comb type damage caused by paint drying in the hairs, near the ferrule.

Straightening Curved Hairs

If you left a brush standing on its hairs in water, or cramped it in storage so that the hairs are now permanently curved in one direction, there is an easy remedy. Dip the hairs (not the ferrule) quickly in and out of very hot water. (The brush hairs are held in the ferrule with glue that could loosen in hot water, resulting in a hairless brush.) Repeat as necessary until the hairs are straight. Then stroke the brush on a damp bar of soap and shape the hairs. This hot-water dip will not straighten fuzzy, every-which-way curls that result from misuse, rough surfaces, and scrubbing.

Which Brush Should You Use?

Ideal brush sizes are suggested for each lesson. If you have not accumulated a range of sizes yet, substitute the largest brushes you can comfortably handle for the ones suggested. If you enlarge or reduce the patterns, then the "ideal" brush sizes would need to be adjusted to correspond. Just remember, though, that the magic is not in a given brush size but rather in your technique.

Brush Size

If you are using a different brand, there may be some variation between my brush sizes and yours. For example, your size No. 6 may not be the same size as my No. 6. So use my recommendations only as a suggestion, and be guided more by what feels comfortable to you. Just be aware that in the beginning, you will probably choose a slightly smaller brush size than would be most expedient. Try to always use the largest brush you can comfortably handle in any given area. It's more efficient, and you're less likely to fidget your painting to death the way you might using a too-small brush. This is true, also, if you're starting with just the three flat brushes listed as basic supplies. Use a brush size suitable to the size of area you are to paint. You wouldn't use a liner brush to paint a 4" area. Sizes of brushes range in number size with generally the smallest to the largest numerically (i.e., No. 12 flat is larger than a No. 2 flat).

1   2   3   4   5   6

When your brushes look like this, here's what you're doing wrong: (1) Handles split, peel, and wobble when they're allowed to soak in water. (2) Acrylic paint will harden in a brush that is not properly cleaned. (3) Hairs bend in storage or when carelessly left standing in water. (4) Comb-like separation of hairs is caused by dried paint. (5) Tunneling effect is caused by paint hardening near the ferrule. (6) Curling hairs result from rough treatment and rough surfaces.

Brush Style

As a general rule, you will use flat brushes to undercoat, to apply washes and sideloaded and doubleloaded strokes, to highlight and shade, and, sometimes, to apply drybrushed effects. Use the liner and round brushes to paint thin lines and small details. Sometimes I will suggest you use a flat brush for some details (such as veins of leaves) just to keep them from looking too stiff and artificial. Highlights painted with the corner of the flat brush look softer and more natural than the precise, hard little dots applied with the liner brush. Narrow, straight lines can also be painted with the chisel edge of the flat brush when it is held perpendicular to the painting surface. Such lines are softer and less defined than those made with the liner brush. Use the round brushes for painting particular strokes, such as for forming seeds, flower petals, and textured citrus flesh. Use an old, splayed brush (flat or round) with hairs sticking in all directions—we'll call it a "scruffy" or "ratty" brush—to apply drybrushed effects and techniques like stippling, pouncing, and others as instructed.

To Trash or Not to Trash?

Damaged brushes are still usable, but not for careful blending techniques and precise strokes. They are handy tools for creating special effects. Instead of using a good brush for drybrushing, scumbling, pouncing, spackling, streaking, or dabbing, grab one of these scruffy or ratty brushes. They're also handy when small children and grandchildren want to paint with you. You can enjoy the painting session without worrying about the damage being done to your good brushes.

BRUSH-LOADING TECHNIQUES

This section explains four methods of loading paint into your brush: full loading, sideloading, doubleloading, and drybrushing. Each technique yields different effects, so it is important to be familiar with all four. Because sideloading is the loading technique that stumps the greatest number of students, I have included especially detailed instructions. Don't be intimidated though; once you have mastered the technique, you can accomplish the loading quickly and efficiently, without having to think about it.

Full Loading

Fully loading the brush.

A fully loaded brush is a brush loaded almost to the metal ferrule with paint generally the thickness it comes from the container. To load the brush, stroke it at the edge of a puddle of paint, working the paint well up into the hairs. Merely dipping the brush in the paint and letting paint cling to the outermost hairs is not fully loading the brush. We will use a fully loaded brush primarily for opaque or textured undercoats.

Sideloading

Sideloading the brush.

A sideloaded stroke should show a gradual (left), not abrupt (right), change in color.

A sideloaded brush is loaded along one edge with color that gradually fades to little or no color on the other edge. We'll call the edges the "paint edge" and the "water edge," respectively. A sideloaded brush produces strokes of shaded color. Such strokes facilitate the application of thin layers of paint for creating highlights, shadows, and delicate accents of color (such as tinges of red, orange, yellow, blue, and purple on leaves). By loading the brush so the water edge stays fairly free of pigment, we can use that edge to nudge or soften the sideloaded application if necessary, or to smooth a too-obvious edge of paint.

One of the most common mistakes in sideloading is not working enough paint up into the hairs of the brush. A few jabs at the paint puddle and a couple of blending strokes on the palette do not properly and sufficiently fill the brush and distribute the paint. A stroke applied with an inadequately prepared brush will have an area of thick paint laying abruptly next to a swath of water, which will quickly evaporate, leaving a hard-edged stripe of paint where you were hoping for a gradual blending of tone. A well-loaded brush, on the other hand, will produce several, nicely gradated strokes with just an occasional remoistening with water or painting medium. On your first read-through of the directions, have a flat brush, palette, paper towel, and water handy. Go through the motions as you read, substituting just water for paint. This will help embed the process in your mind before you get down to working with the paint.

1. While it is possible to sideload a variety of brush styles, develop your skill by practicing with a flat brush in excellent condition. At first, work with a No. 8, 10, or 12 brush. As your skill develops, try the smaller flat brushes.
2. Dip the brush in clean water. (If you're using oil paints, dip the brush in painting medium.) Shake off the excess; then blot the entire length of hairs, on one side only, on a paper towel. Watch the hairs, and as the wet shine disappears, immediately lift the brush. Do not blot the other side. The water or medium remaining in the brush should provide the right amount of moisture for dispersing the paint. Too much water or medium will make the paint too juicy to control; too little will cause the brush to drag and skip.

3. Pick up a little paint on the corner of the slightly damp brush.

4. Stroke the brush back and forth on the palette in a short space (no longer than an inch; even shorter for smaller brushes). Stroke over and over in the same spot, picking up more paint as needed to completely load the hairs on one side of the brush. Moving to a different clean spot on the palette with every stroke (a common mistake) will use up the paint rather than force it to load well up into the hairs of the brush.

5. Continue to add more paint, a little at a time, until color is worked almost up to the metal ferrule. Avoid loading too much paint at once since doing so will make your blending area messy. It may also make the paint spread too far across the brush, eliminating the clear water edge. Too much paint loaded at once can also force paint into the ferrule area, making brush cleaning a hassle.

6. As you stroke the brush on the palette, stroke on both the top and underside of the hairs. If you stroke only the bottom side, you will be pushing the paint up toward the top side of the hairs and it will not be worked properly into the hairs. When you flip the brush to stroke the top side, be sure to align the color edge of the brush with the color stroke on the palette.

7. When you think you have loaded sufficient paint in the brush and have blended it so it progresses from a deep color on the paint edge to a pale color or no color on the water edge, make a short test stroke on a clean spot on your palette. The stroke should show a gradual change in color.

8. If the color in your stroke changes abruptly, you need to blend on the palette a little more to distribute the paint gradually across the hairs. Try this: "Walk" the brush gradually away from the edge of the paint. If the paint is on the left edge of the brush, walk toward the right by making short strokes parallel to the original stroke, like a series of stripes. Then walk back toward the left, applying pressure on the brush while stroking, gobbling up the trail of stripes. At first, walk only half the width of the hairs of the brush until you are proficient at picking up—on the way back—all the paint deposited while walking away. Walk on both sides of the brush.

9. Another way to soften the abrupt color change in the brush, whether side- or doubleloaded (see below), is to stroke the brush on the palette, moving like a downhill slalom racer in slow motion. Stroke back and forth in this wiggly fashion several times.Then, on the same spot, finish with several straight strokes, stroking on both the top and underside of the hairs. The wiggle will help move the concentrated paint on the edge of the brush across the hairs.

10. If the paint drags a little, at any time, dip the water edge of the brush into a drop of water or medium and blot the excess. (I like to keep a large drop on my palette so it's easier to see and control how much moisture my brush picks up.) You can also use a bottle cap or a palette cup. Blend on the previous stroking area on the palette to distribute the moisture across the brush hairs.

"Walking" the brush away from the paint puddle.

Whoops!

If you accidently get strong color (or in the case of doubleloading, the wrong color) across the entire brush at any time, you need not rinse the brush entirely and start over. Just dip the edge of the brush that was supposed to remain clear into a droplet of water or medium, wipe the paint off by pulling that edge through a paper towel held between your thumb and forefinger. Then pick up a little more moisture, blot it, and continue stroking and loading the brush.

Stroking the brush in a "slalom" motion.

Doubleloading

A doubleloaded brush is loaded with two different colors or values, one on each edge. After blending the doubleloaded colors on the palette, the brush produces a stroke having three colors or values—two from the two colors loaded onto the edges of the brush and the third as a result of the two colors mixing together in the middle of the brush. The gradation of color in a doubleloaded brush makes possible the application of subtle color transitions such as in painting highlights, reflected lights, and shadow areas. The effect is slightly different from using a sideloaded brush: The color application will be more opaque, and can appear too heavy and flat if not applied thinly over previous thin-layered areas.

To doubleload the flat brush, follow the procedure for sideloading the brush, except in step 3, pick up a different color on each corner of the brush. In the test stroke you make in step 7, you should see the color from one edge of the brush gradate gradually into the color on the other edge. For example, if you loaded yellow on one edge and blue on the other, the colors should merge into green across the center of the brush. If there is an empty space in the middle or a sharp edge where one color abuts another, you haven't blended the colors sufficiently in the brush. Go on to step 8 and/or step 9, being careful not to "walk" or "zig" the brush so far as to let the yellow edge, for example, walk or zig into the blue paint, and vice versa. You will be able to walk only short distances before retracing your steps; the object being to keep the colors on the edges of the brush as pure as possible, while merging the colors in the middle.

If you need to remoisten the brush as in step 10, you can pick up water or medium sparsely on either edge. Just be sure to blot the brush before stroking on the palette to continue to blend, or the paint will puddle and you'll lose the distinct colors on the edges.

Doubleloaded brush before blending.

A doubleloaded brush stroke should show a gradual (left), not abrupt (right), change in color where in the two colors meet.

Whoops!

If you do lose one color, for example the yellow, it's not necessary to rinse the brush and start over completely. Moisten a small section of a paper towel, and holding it between your thumb and forefinger, pull the yellow paint edge of the brush through. Wipe off the "tainted" yellow leaving the green and blue intact. Then reload the yellow (and blue if neccessary) and proceed with the blending.

Brush Blending on the Palette

Palette knife blending, in which two or more colors are mixed together using a palette knife, is perhaps the most familiar way of mixing different color paints. You can also mix colors by picking up on the brush a little of each color desired in the mixture and stroking—but not stirring—them together on the palette. If we avoid overmixing the colors, thereby creating one bland tone, we will have lively mixed colors that retain traces of the original hues. (Palette knife mixing can also yield the same results if not overdone.) In using such a mixture, we would most often work with a fully loaded brush.

Palette-knife blending.

Brush blending.

Basic Brushstrokes

Here are seven basic brushstrokes that will help you complete the worksheets in this book. Practice each one on scrap paper until you get the hang of it before taking it to your composition.

Knife of Chisel (flat brush)

Skim the knife or chisel edge of the brush along the surface to form a thin line. Be sure to keep the brush perpendicular for the best control and narrowest line.

Broad (flat brush)

Maintaining even pressure, pull a stroke using the full width of the flat brush. Pull the brush back to a chisel edge, standing it up perpendicular to the painting surface, leaving a clean, even edge.

Comma (round brush)

Head

Tail

While loading the brush, flatten the tip of the hairs and scoop up a little extra paint. For a streaky comma stroke, load the brush with one color, then tap the excess off the tip; do not wipe it off. Dip the brush in a second color, then tap it slightly to merge the colors.

1 Lean the brush handle slightly back in your hand. Press the brush down, letting the hairs flair out to form the rounded head.

2 Pull the stroke, gradually releasing pressure on the brush and letting the hairs return to a point.

3 Pull the stroke to a fine point, standing the brush perpendicular to the painting surface. Stop, then lift off.

Flat Comma (flat brush)

This stroke is created from head to tail. The brush starts at 12 o'clock. It should rotate gradually to about 2 o'clock; then stop rotating as you slide the complete stroke, pulling the tail toward 7 or 8 o'clock.

1 Press the brush down and begin pulling a flat stroke.

2 Continue pulling while releasing pressure and curving the stroke slightly. Let the handle lean into the curve.

3 Continue releasing pressure and pulling until the brush comes to the chisel edge. Stop and lift off.

Teardrop (round brush)

Tail

Head

This stroke is the reverse of the comma stroke: It begins skinny and ends fat. For a two-toned teardrop, load the brush with one color, then wipe the tip. Load the tip with a second color. Paint the teardrop. The last color loaded on the brush will form the teardrop's tail, the first will be found in its head.

1 Begin on the tip of the brush, skimming lightly on the surface to form the tail. For best results in starting a skinny tail, begin the stroke in the air and glide gently onto the surface.

2 Gradually apply pressure while pulling the brush until you've obtained the length or fullness desired.

Come to a complete stop, then stand the brush back up on its tip perpendicular to the surface. Notice that, upon stopping, the tip of the brush is in the middle of the head. Lift off.

Flat S (flat brush)

This stroke is formed by applying and releasing pressure. Your brush should never change direction. Do not rotate it in your fingers or attempt to draw the letter S.

1 Start at 8 o'clock and slide toward 2 o'clock, gradually increasing pressure.

2 Continue to increase pressure as you change direction and head for 5 o'clock. In the middle of the stroke, begin gradually releasing pressure.

3 Continue releasing pressure as you change direction again and head for 2 o'clock, ending on the knife edge of the brush. The legs of the stroke should be parallel and the same length.

Flat Crescent (flat brush)

This stroke requires you to slide and rotate your brush to achieve the thin to thick to thin appearance.

1 Slide on the chisel edge, moving the brush from 6 o'clock straight toward 9 o'clock, and gradually begin applying pressure.

2 Increase pressure as you round the curve, rotating the brush until you are stroking with the bristles flat. Then gradually begin releasing pressure.

3 Continue releasing pressure and pull the brush to the chisel edge. The beginning and ending legs of the stroke should be identical—the same length and width.

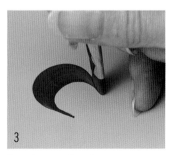

SPECIAL BRUSH TECHNIQUES

Once you are familiar with the different methods of brush-loading, you can use them to create a variety of wonderful effects.

Washes and Floated Colors

A wash (also called a glaze) or floated color is a layer of thin paint usually applied with a flat brush over a dry background or undercoat. You will often see the terms used interchangeably as, indeed, the results are very similar. The paint, thinned with water or water plus a medium is translucent or semi-translucent, thus allowing some of the color of the background or undercoat to shine through. This creates a "glowing-from-within" effect if applied over a light color. When applying a wash (glaze) or floated color, be sure to put it down thinly. Dry it completely with a hair dryer before applying another layer. This will prevent the lifting or dissolving of the previous application. You can build layer upon dry layer until you build up the depth or variety of colors you want.

There are two kinds of washes or glazes: flat and gradated. A *flat wash* creates a thin but uniform color throughout. It is created by fully loading a flat brush with thinned paint. A *gradated wash* is one that progresses from strong to faded color. It is applied by sideloading a flat brush.

Floated color is the application of color over a thin layer of water or water plus medium, which has been applied over a dry undercoat or a base coat. Thus, the color is "floated" across the surface on that layer of moisture. The effect can be flat or gradated. When we work with a sideloaded brush, we are actually floating color across the moisture that the water side of the brush lays down with every stroke made. In this book, I make abundant use of washes and floated colors to build up multiple layers of thin paint; to apply shading and highlighting and accent colors; and to adjust colors or submerge them slightly when needed. I use a sideloaded brush for most of these effects, so be sure to master that brush-loading technique. The results are well worth the effort.

Puddly Wash

The "puddly" wash is, like above, the application of a thin layer of paint over a dry undercoat or background. The exception is that it is applied very juicily. It will take a while longer to dry because there will be little puddles throughout the wash, rather than a smooth, thin layer of colored moisture. The paint pigment collects in varying amounts in the puddles. When the puddles dry, the effect is a splotchy application of thin paint. Wonderful for creating spontaneous-looking, natural effects!

Flat wash.

Gradated wash.

Puddly wash.

Drybrushing

A dry brush is a brush having no moisture added before picking up very little paint, which is then mostly wiped off. A drybrushed stroke produces glittering or scattered touches of colors or highlights, which cling primarily to elevated portions of strokes painted previously.

Any brush can be used for drybrushing; but this is a great way to use your old, scruffy brushes—those that have separated, splayed, and curled, and that have paint dried in the hairs near the ferrule.

1. To load the brush, dip the tip of the dry hairs in a smear of paint on the palette. Work the paint into the hairs by stroking or rubbing the brush on the palette. (This technique can be rough on good brushes, which is why I like to use old, ratty ones!)
2. Then wipe the brush nearly dry on a dry paper towel.
3. Hold the brush parallel to your painting surface and skim lightly across the area you wish to highlight or add broken color to. If you wiped the brush sufficiently dry, you should not see any paint appear on the surface with your first stroke. It should require several passes, and even then the paint should be barely visible. As you become confident that there is barely any paint in the brush, apply more pressure as you stroke. You should have to work at laying down any color. The harder you work, in fact, the more control you have. To avoid being surprised by a too heavy application, lightly pass the brush over some dried paint on your palette to test the amount of paint in the brush.

Applying drybrushed highlights.

Not like this   Like this

If you didn't load the paint sparsely enough, you might lay down an obvious brush stroke rather than barely perceptible glints. Quickly wipe up the paint with a damp towel and dry the area thoroughly; reload the brush and try again. Remember that it's better to apply several inadequate coats, building up to the final desired effect than to apply one, heavy, layer.

Experimenting

Don't be afraid to experiment with different brushes and techniques than those I recommend in the lessons. In working through the lessons, you will see that, in painting leaf veins, for example, I have suggested a variety of approaches:

· Using the liner brush.
· Using a sideloaded flat brush.
· Using overlapping, sideloaded strokes to soften the previously painted stroke.
· Painting V-shaped marks to indicate veins.
· Using the chisel edge of the flat brush.
· Using a combination of techniques and brushes.

Try all the variations, then determine the brush and technique that works best for you. My goal is to assure you that there is no one "right" way of doing things. There are many ways to achieve the effects we seek. Have fun testing them all!

Scumbling

To scumble paint into an area is to apply it randomly in broken, overlapping patches, somewhat like crosshatching. Scumbling is a convenient way of unifying subject colors in a composition by introducing them into the background or into other areas. I usually like to soften the edges of my scumbled strokes so they don't draw too much attention to themselves. If the scumbling is done wet into wet paint, the edges of brush strokes soften readily. If the scumbling is done wet onto dry paint, it may be necessary to overstroke with a little of the original background color, thinned, to soften brush stroke edges. Scumbling can be done with a fully loaded, a sideloaded, a doubleloaded, or a (nearly) dry brush, depending upon the color(s) being used, how much of it is wanted, and the effect desired.

Lifting Out Highlights

After applying a wash or floated color, you can lift out some of the still damp color to expose more of the light undercoat. Use a damp cotton swab or clean damp brush. This must be done quickly, before the layer starts to set up, so have your brush or cotton swab already dampened (not dripping) with clean water.

Edge-to-Edge Blending

To add highlighting, shading, or accent colors in the middle of an area and to avoid having a hard edge of color, use edge-to-edge blending. This can be done with either a sideloaded or doubleloaded brush.

To blend edge-to-edge with a sideloaded brush, first slightly dampen the area to be highlighted with a painting medium plus water. Place the paint edge of the brush to the center of the area to be highlighted and blend it outward, leading with the water edge. Then quickly return to the starting point, reverse the brush, again placing the paint edge to the center of the highlight area; and this time blend in the other direction, leading with the water edge.

To blend edge to edge with a doubleloaded brush, follow the process above, omitting the layer of moisture. I generally use the doubleloaded brush if I wish to highlight or shade something that is painted opaquely. However, for working on subjects built up with thin washes and floated colors, I prefer the transparency of a sideloaded brush.

Scumbling.

Using a cotton swab to lift out highlights.

Edge-to-edge blending with doubleloaded brush.

Edge-to-edge blending with sideloaded brush.

Transferring Patterns

Each step-by-step lesson includes one or more patterns for you to paint from. To transfer a design onto your painting surface, first copy it onto tracing paper. (I like to use a thin, felt tip marker such as a Sanford Ultra Fine Point Sharpie or a Pigma Micron.) Then use one of the methods described below to transfer the design. Try them all, and use the one that best suits your needs at a given time.

Retracing Pattern Lines

Turn your traced design over, and on the back side retrace your pattern lines using a chalk pencil or a regular graphite pencil. Position the twice-traced pattern, chalk- or pencil-side down, on your surface. Retrace lightly over the felt tip drawn lines using a stylus or a "dead" ballpoint pen. Avoid heavy pressure. You want to transfer just a faint line of chalk or graphite from the back of the pattern, not dig a ditch in your painting surface.

Chalk or Pencil Rubbing

Turn your traced design over and rub the back side of the pattern area with the side of a piece of cheap chalkboard chalk or the graphite from a No. 2 (or softer) pencil, held almost parallel to the paper. Shake off excess chalk or graphite. Lay the coated side face down on your surface and retrace gently over your pattern lines to transfer the design. Be careful not to rub your hand over the design as the pressure will transfer smudges of chalk or graphite to your surface.

Commercial Transfer Papers

Purchase a package of artists' transfer paper, such as Chacopaper. These papers are designed specifically for use with artists' materials. Do not use regular office carbon paper as it will bleed through your paints and spoil your painting. Artists' transfer papers are available in gray, white, blue, red, and blue-green, depending on the manufacturer and available in the Fine Arts section in an art, craft, or hobby store. Position the transfer paper between your pattern and your painting surface, making sure the coated side is face down on the painting surface.

When new, the coating on the purchased transfer papers (as well as on the homemade ones described below) is heavy and will transfer a line that is much too thick, so use a light touch in working with them. I like to wipe over the coated side of commercial transfer papers with a paper towel before using them the first time to remove excess coating.

Make Your Own Transfer Paper

Rub the back of a sheet of thin tracing paper with the side of a piece of chalk or with a No. 2 (or softer) pencil, held almost parallel to the paper. Cover your fingertips with a piece of chamois cloth or paper towel and rub the chalk or graphite into the paper. Shake off excess chalk or graphite dust. Fold the coated paper in half, treated side in, for storage.

Whoops!

Avoid frustration! Pay close attention when positioning the transfer paper beneath your pattern and on your painting surface in preparation for transferring your design. It's too easy to place the transfer paper upside down; and if you don't make a habit of checking your progress after copying the first line or two, you might discover after a long, tedious tracing session that you've transferred the entire pattern onto the back of your original pattern. It is helpful to write on the transfer paper in felt tip marker, "This side up!" Or write your name, or draw a smiley face. Do something to remind yourself to be alert.

The Color Wheel

The color wheel is a wonderful and convenient way to study colors; to see how they are related to one another; and to see how they can be mixed from—and with—one another.

Seeing the colors arranged around a wheel also makes it easier to imagine, to study, and to create color schemes.

How the Color Wheel Works

For now, let's take a look at how a color wheel is created. The artist's (or pigment) color wheel is based on three primary colors—red, blue, and yellow—which are the basis for creating all other colors. We cannot create our three pure primary colors by mixing together any of our other pigments; we have to buy the primaries. But from those three purchased colors we can mix a wide range of hues. You can see eighteen of those hues on the intermediary color wheel on the following page. If we created gradual gradations between all of the colors on this wheel as well as on the tertiary color wheel, and then created nine additional values by adding black and white to every mixture on the wheel creating shades and tints; and then mixed nine more values of gray, to create tones, and added them to every color as well—wow! Can you imagine how many colors we could create just from our three primaries plus black and white? Hundreds! And what if we bought additional primary reds, blues, and yellows and mixed a color wheel with them, adding the blacks and whites; and then recombined the assorted primaries so we used different reds, yellows, and blues together. We could mix, literally, millions of colors. It boggles the brain! The color wheels on pages 24 and 25 give a small idea of what happens when we interchange primary colors.

Paint Your Own Color Wheel

To mix colors for your first color wheel, try to use the clearest, purest red, yellow, and blue you can find. Otherwise, you may end up with some colors that are a little disappointing if they're not what you hope or expect to get. For example, there are reds that have a slight orangish cast. If you mix them with blue to make a violet, you will get a brownish violet. And it will be even more brown if the blue you use has a slightly greenish cast. In both cases, even though you are mixing only two paints (red and blue) you are actually mixing all three primary colors together because both the orangish red and the greenish blue already have yellow in them. While the mixture may not be exactly what you had hoped for, it will still be a lively color (a tertiary color, in fact, so called because it includes all three primary colors). It can be an excellent shading and toning color, with much more life to

it than using a premixed brown or a black, which tends to deaden colors.

On a piece of sturdy paper (watercolor paper, poster board, or Bristol board) draw a circle about 7 inches in diameter. Divide your circle evenly into twelve pie-shaped segments and write in numerals as on a clock face. Now you're ready to paint your color wheel as shown on the next page. Each time you mix two colors together for the color wheel, try to create a color that appears visually to be exactly halfway between the two colors used in the mixture. For example, in mixing red and blue to make violet, be sure the violet does not appear more red or more blue, but rather just pure violet. It may be hard to see what color you have since it will be very dark. Spread a little of the mixture thinly on your white palette paper to check it before adding it to your color wheel. If it's too reddish, add more blue, and vice versa. Remember: Adding a medium to your paints will prolong their drying time.

Imagine the color wheel to be like the face of a clock. We'll use the three primary colors (at twelve, four, and eight o'clock) to mix colors to cover all the remaining numerals, and then some!

Primary Colors

In painting, the three primary colors are always red, blue, and yellow. To create our color wheel, we'll use the following DecoArt Americana acrylic paints:

· Primary Red
· True Blue
· Yellow Light

Note that other disciplines work with different sets of primary colors. For example, printers use cyan, magenta, and yellow. Physicists, working with lights, use green, blue, and red as their primary colors, mixing these to create the remaining spectrum colors.

The primary colors cannot be mixed; they must be purchased. Place them on the twelve, four, and eight as shown. The primary colors are red, blue, and yellow.

The secondary colors are created by mixing any two primary colors, and are placed between those two primaries (on the remaining even clock numerals). The secondary colors are orange (red + yellow), green (blue + yellow), and violet (red + blue).

The intermediary colors lie in between the primary and adjacent secondary colors with which they are mixed. The intermediary colors are yellow-green (yellow + green), green-yellow (green + yellow), green-blue (green + blue), blue-green (blue + green), blue-violet (blue + violet), violet-blue (violet + blue), violet-red (violet + red), red-violet (red + violet), red-orange (red + orange), orange-red (orange + red), orange-yellow (orange + yellow), and yellow-orange (yellow + orange).

The tertiary colors are created by mixing any two secondary colors; thus each tertiary color includes all three primary colors. Tertiary colors include, among others, citrine (orange + green, thus [red + yellow] + [blue + yellow]), russet (orange + violet, thus [red + yellow] + [red + blue]), and olive (green + orange, thus [yellow + blue] + [yellow + red]). We can also mix subtle variations.

Hint

When creating intermediary colors, mix two variations (as I did above): one having more of the primary color, the other having more of the secondary color. Put both mixtures in a single space on the odd clock numerals (for example, yellow-green at one o'clock, close to the yellow; green-yellow also at one o'clock, close to the green.) The first color in the compound name is predominant in the mixture.

Color Wheel Variations

Each primary color affects all the colors between it and the next primary color. For example, we find red in the mixtures on the three clock numerals both between red and yellow and between red and blue. Look what happens when we exchange our pure primary colors (red, yellow, and blue) with ones that are slightly different.

Note that I have not divided the intermediary colors into two portions on these wheels. You can imagine how the colors on the odd clock numeral spaces would look if each half of the color had a little more of its neighboring color added to it.

After painting your pure primaries color wheel, make additional wheels substituting different reds, yellows, and blues. Jot notes on the colors you used. That way, if you don't have a color suggested for a particular lesson, you'll have a record of how to mix something close.

Color wheel created from three pure primary colors for comparison.

Here I replaced the primary blue with a blue having a slight greenish cast. The red and yellow remain the same. Observe how the different blue affects all the colors from one o'clock through seven o'clock.

In this color wheel I substituted a soft, muted yellow for the original bright yellow. The red and blue remain the same. Notice how the yellow has affected the three colors on either side of it. Half of our color wheel now is pastel, and the other half contains intense, deep colors. We may want to add a touch of white or creamy yellow to the lower half of the wheel to both tint and lower the intensity of the remaining colors.

Here I kept the original blue and yellow and changed the red. Now we have lovely muted reds, oranges, and violets. If we add to the blue and yellow—and their mixtures—a little of their complementary colors (more about them, soon), the entire color wheel would be made up of low intensity, but lovely, colors.

I replaced all three primary colors in this color wheel. Look at the violet mixtures at five, six, and seven o'clock. They are very grayed. And little wonder: Both the red and the blue contain a good bit of yellow. Thus, when mixing the red and blue to get violet, we've also included the third primary color, yellow; and three primaries mixed together result in a dull, low intensity tertiary color. But doesn't the entire color palette look interesting?

This figure shows another lovely, muted palette. All three of these primary colors are different from our original three. These three primaries give us deep, rich mixtures.

COMPLEMENTARY COLORS

Now let's see what exciting things happen in the world of color when we take some of our mixed colors and mix *them* together. Colors that are located directly opposite each other on the color wheel are called "complementary colors." Look at your color wheel or the one on page 24 (use the one made up of pure primary colors). What color is directly across from yellow? from blue? from red-orange? If you answered violet, orange, and green-blue, respectively, you get a smiley face. It's good to learn, early on, what the complement is of every color. That knowledge enables us to mix beautifully subdued colors, to place certain colors adjacent to others in our painting for strong impact, and to create engaging color schemes.

Finding Complements

A pair of complementary colors consists of all three primary colors: red, blue, yellow. Choose one of the three primaries (for example, red). To determine its complement, mentally mix the remaining two primaries together (blue + yellow = green).

Therefore, the complement of red
is blue + yellow and vice versa.

Likewise, the complement of
blue + red is yellow and vice versa.

Remembering Complements

Until you have memorized the locations of colors around the color wheel, or the pairs of complementary colors, here are some memory aids and interesting facts to help you.

- An aid to memorizing the complementary colors—
  think of the holidays:
- Christmas—red and green
- Easter—violet and yellow
- Halloween—orange (pumpkin) and blue (sky)

- The complement of a primary color is always a secondary color and vice versa. Don't just take my word for it. Look at the color wheel and check it out.
- The complement of a cool color is always a warm color and vice versa. We'll explore temperature shortly. Just remember to come back to this statement and check it out on your color wheel, as well.
- The complement of a color can be found in its *afterimage*. If all else fails, stare at the color you need to know the complement of until your eyes start to fatigue. (Allow about 20 seconds or so. You'll see a slight, white halo appear around the color and your eyes may feel like they're crossing or looking right through the color.) Then shift your gaze to a white piece of paper or wall. After several seconds, you will see a faint afterimage in the complementary color. It takes some folks a while to learn to see the afterimage, so if you're not successful right away, don't give up. It's fun to do, and you can practice it anywhere, even in a crowd or during a boring meeting. No one will ever know!

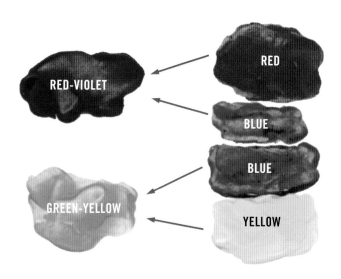

Finding the complement of red-violet.

Complementary Colors Do Neat Things!

Placing complementary colors side by side intensifies them, each one enhancing the other. Mixing complementary colors together neutralizes them, creating low intensity, subdued, grayed colors.

You can use both of the above attributes together to make your paintings really pop. Say you plan to paint an orange pumpkin. Put it on a blue background to enhance the orange. If you mix a little orange into the blue to subdue the background, its dullness will make the pumpkin appear even brighter.

The conscious use of complementary colors plays such an important role in our paintings that we will visit them again when we explore attributes of color such as value, intensity, and temperature later in this section; and when we discuss creating color schemes. If you don't quite get it yet, just review these pages once in a while. It *will* begin to make sense.

Notice how the violet and yellow swatches are intensified by their proximity to each other.

Cover up the colors on the left side of this page, then stare at the blue ball above. Next, quickly shift your gaze to the empty box below for a few seconds and wait for the afterimage to appear. What color is the ball? What color are the stripes?

Violet and yellow combined become gray.

PLAYING IN THE MUD

Just imagine all the different colors of mud there must be around the world. Wonderful colors. Yet, when we mix a color that disappoints us, we often call it "mud." Well, it's time we showed a little more appreciation for these beautifully subdued, low intensity colors. They have oodles of uses in our paintings. They can actually save a painting from becoming a hodge podge of too many active colors trying to show off how pretty each is. They can unify a painting that looks like a jumble of unrelated things with not a thread to hold it all together. But we need to understand how those subdued colors happen, and how we can control them; making them happen when we want, and how we want them, and preventing them from happening when we don't want them.

If you've been reading carefully and thinking about what we've covered so far, you know that creating those low intensity colors involves mixing all three primary colors together. When one or two of the three primaries predominate in the mixture, we call it a tertiary color, which is, indeed, what we get when we mix two complementary colors together. When all three primaries are in approximately equal visual amounts, it's hard to distinguish any particular color. (Alright, it looks like mud.)

We can learn tremendous color mixing lessons from working with a pile of muddy looking paint. So let's play in the mud.

1. Squeeze out a bit of all three primary colors and add some medium to prolong their drying time. Then, mix them together. Now, let's try to adjust the color of the pile of paint to make a rich, dark, neutral gray. But first, we need to see exactly what color we're starting with. Depending

upon the intensity of your paints, you may have a very dark pile of paint there.

2. With your finger or a palette knife, drag a small amount of paint from the edge of the pile. Mix a little white into it. This will make it easier to see what color is predominant in the mixture.

3. Now add a little of that color's complementary color. If the color smear is a brownish red, mix a very small amount of green into the pile. Then test it again. If the smear looks more bluish, mix in blue's complementary color, orange. And so on. Keep working until you create a gray that appears perfectly neutral—not too red, not too blue, not too violet, orange, yellow, or green. Think about every addition you make to be sure you're adding the complementary color. And, add it sparingly, testing with white on a small smear after each addition. Don't just carelessly dump colors in the pile. You won't learn a thing but how to make that proverbial mud. Instead, make a conscious effort to understand what's happening, and to study each variation of gray you mix. You will see some gorgeous colors when you stretch them out with a little white. You might even want to save swatches of the mixtures to remind you later of the lovely grays you're capable of mixing. Don't just read about it, do it! It's the only way you'll learn.

Hint

If you're painting a composition you wish to appear warm, try mixing a little reddish-gray with all the hues you use in that painting. Use the bluish-grays to create a cooler impression. If there is something in the painting you really want to stand out, do not mix the gray into its colors. The contrast of intense colors against the slightly grayed colors will put that subject in the spotlight!

You can create an array of lovely neutrals from a seemingly dull pile of "mud."

THE FOUR PROPERTIES OF COLOR

There are four properties of color, which we need to understand in order to use color successfully in our paintings.

They are:

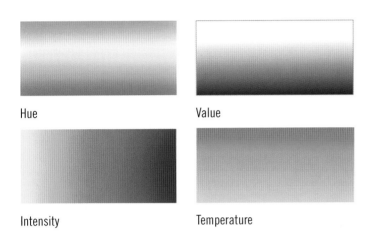

Hue

Value

Intensity

Temperature

Hue

Hue is simply another word for color. What hue is it? What color is it? We have already discussed the names of the spectral hues in our study of the color wheel. Those names, combined with the other properties we're about to explore, will help us to accurately describe any particular color.

Value

Value refers to the lightness or darkness of a hue—its relationship to white, black, and the grays in between. For example, pink is a light value hue; burgundy is a dark value hue. The American portrait painter and teacher Albert H. Munsell (1858–1918) determined there were nine distinct, equidistant steps of gray between black and white. The value scale he originated bears his name.

Tints, Shades, and Tones

By adding white or black, we can raise or lower the value of any hue. The addition of white raises the value and creates a *tint*. The addition of black lowers the value and creates a *shade*. Adding a mixture of black plus white creates a grayed *tone*. A tone can also have nine values; more black in the gray mixture would make it a lower value; more white, a higher value.

Effects of Surrounding Values

Take a look at the value scale at right, paying particular attention to the dots. At first glance, it appears that the dots grow lighter as they proceed down the scale. Wrong! After I finished painting the nine equidistant steps of gray, I took a bit of the middle value gray (No. 5) and painted a dot of that value on each step of the scale. This is a

reminder that every hue and value we paint is affected by the hue and value we paint around it. If we paint something dark next to a light object, it will make the light object seem even lighter. Sometimes in painting, if we can't seem to get our lights light enough, we must switch our attention to the darks and push them darker. The contrast will make the lights appear lighter. This effect of contrasts also works with intensity and temperature, which we'll explore shortly.

HIGH VALUES		
LIGHT VALUES	WHITE	●
	9	●
	8	●
	7	●
MEDIUM VALUES	6	●
	5	●
	4	●
DARK VALUES	3	●
	2	●
	1	●
	BLACK	●
LOW VALUES		

The Munsell value scale specifies nine equal and equidistant steps of gray between pure black and pure white. Pure black is placed at the bottom of the Munsell value scale, and is designated as 0. Each addition of white or light color to that pure black would raise its value upward on the scale. Munsell determined that mixing black and white together would produce nine different shades of gray, each the same interval apart from their neighbors. The numbers simply indicate the position on the scale: The higher the number, the lighter the value.

Value and the Color Wheel

Refer to the basic color wheel on page 24 and compare the positions of the pure hues as they progress down the wheel. Notice that the lightest hue, yellow, is at the top of the wheel, and would be near the top of the value scale. The medium value hues—oranges and greens—are midway down the wheel and the scale, followed by the somewhat darker hues, red and blue. Finally, the violets or purples, our dark value hues, are at the bottom of the wheel and also the value scale. Make a black and white photocopy of your color wheel and check this out.

Adjusting Values

Thankfully, the hues don't have to remain in the positions (just described) on the value scale. We can adjust any of the hues and move them up or down the value scale by adding a little of a hue that is above or below it on the color wheel. We can move the hues even higher, to the top of the value scale, by mixing them with plenty of white. Likewise, we can move hues further down the value scale by adding black. We just must realize that the hue may shift. For example, black added to yellow will turn it a greenish hue. To keep yellow in the yellow family, we would need to lower its value with brown, or with its complement, violet. Likewise adding white to hues can sometimes make them look chalky. For instance, adding white to red results in a sugary pink. If you want a light red, instead of "cotton candy pink," add a bit of yellow with the white to lighten the red.

The Key to a Painting

Key is a word that describes a collection of related values. Just as a piece of music is said to be in a minor or a major key, or in the key of C or F—in other words composed of a collection of related notes or tones—a painting is also described as being in a certain key. A *full key* painting uses all nine values on the scale plus black and white. A *high key* painting uses just the values on the upper part of the scale plus white. A *low key* painting uses just the values on the lower part of the scale plus black. A *middle key* painting uses just the values in the middle of the scale.

When we look at a painting, our first perception is its lightness or darkness. From that initial, brief glimpse—even before noting the subject matter—we may develop an impression or have an emotional reaction to the painting. Think of a favorite painting. Determine its overall lightness or darkness. Now imagine it painted in different values. A high key painting (that originally appeared cheerful, bright, and positive) becomes ponderous, heavy, mysterious, maybe oppressive when shifted to the lower, darker values.

Now imagine the most depressed scene you can. You would probably paint that scene in predominately dark hues, and grays and blacks. Slide that same mental picture up the value scale and the immediate reaction (until the subject matter was recognized) would not be one of gloom. Noting the light values of the hues, the viewer would expect a more lighthearted theme. Once the response to the lightness or

darkness of the painting has registered, then the viewer must reconcile it with the emotional response to the painting's content. We have power over how the viewer responds to our paintings, but we have to know how to use that power to accomplish our purposes in creating the painting.

The same painting in four different keys. From left to right: full key, high key, low key, and middle key.

Intensity

Intensity refers to the brightness or dullness of a hue and is sometimes called its "chroma" or "saturation." Intense color is fully saturated, pure, strong, brilliant, and unaltered by the addition of other pigments. Used thoughtfully, a very intense hue surrounded by hues of lesser intensity can be riveting. Beware, though, that the use of too many fully saturated hues in a painting can be disconcerting and can weaken it.

Lowering Intensity

Mixing complementary colors together neutralizes the colors or lowers their intensity. An easy and effective way of lowering the intensity of color is to mix it with a little of its complementary color (the color opposite it on the color wheel). In a yellow apple, for example, you can lower the intensity of the yellow by mixing in violet for its shadow areas. Remember that a pair of complementary colors, between them, contains all three primary hues. And when all three primaries are mixed together (in equal amounts) we get a neutral color.

Increasing Intensity

Placing complementary colors side by side intensifies their colors. Placing a fully saturated color beside—or surrounded by—its complementary color, which has been lowered in intensity, makes the saturated color appear even brighter. So if you've painted a red apple and you want it to nearly "pop" out of the painting, surround it with a green of lowered intensity.

Understanding how great a role intensity can play in our painting helps us use it effectively both to accentuate the focal point and to lead the viewer's gaze.

High Intensity

Low Intensity

Neutral

Low Intensity

High Intensity

Mixing a color with its complement lowers its intensity. On either end of the neutral color in this mixture, we can see the gradually lowered intensities of the red and the green. Use your hands to cover all but a small section of the strip as you study it.

The same bright red has been placed on three different colored backgrounds. Notice how those surrounding colors affect the red. The bright green (top) competes with the red for attention. The green's intensity almost makes the red appear dull. The low intensity green (middle) makes the red appear intense. That bright red all but disappears, however, when placed on its neighboring color, orange (bottom).

Temperature

Temperature refers to the suggestive effect of warmness or coolness of a hue. Warm colors (red-violets, reds, oranges, yellows with a slight orange cast) seem to advance, or come forward. They are energetic, agitated, passionate, athletic, reminiscent of fire, sun, and heat. Cool colors (blue-violets, blues, greens, and yellows with a slight green cast) seem to recede, or move away. They are quiet, pastoral, restful, reminiscent of sky, water, distance, and open space. Understanding colors' advancing and receding effects further enhances our ability to manipulate colors to suit our purpose in a painting.

Relating to the Color Wheel

Look at the color wheel. If you draw a line through the diameter of the circle, slicing into the yellow and the violet, the hues to the left of the line are warm colors; those to the right of the line are cool colors. The yellow and violet are just about neutral in temperature; but they can be easily shifted from warm to cool by the slight addition of an intermediary hue to either side of them.

Now, notice what happens when we select the complement of a color: The complement of a warm color is a cool color; and, conversely, the complement of a cool color is a warm one. You will notice that in each pair of complementary colors there is a warm and a cool color. Check it out on the color wheel.

Paint a Mental Picture

Suppose you wanted to paint a brass vase full of yellow tulips. How would you work with temperature (as well as, of course, with intensity, value, and hue)? Consider how you might treat the background to show off the tulips. What hue and what kind of texture would you choose? Would you make the background warm or cool? With what? Would you warm the yellow of the tulips? How? The brass vase, if you let it reflect all the wonderful hues surrounding it, could steal the show from the tulips. How could you make the tulips more eye-catching? Lots to think about!

Hopefully by now you can think in artistic terms, which should give you a bit of confidence. Don't worry if you don't master it all right away. Just keep reviewing the material and trying to sort out the possibilities every time you paint. Make a point of trying to describe hues, when thinking or speaking of them, in terms of their value, intensity, and temperature, rather than in the clever names manufacturers give them—like "purple passion fantasy," and "desert grass green." To tell a friend we painted a room "toasted persimmon" would leave the friend wondering: What hue does a persimmon turn when it's toasted? Is the room now a bright orange, a deep, dark orange, a brown? But if we say the hue is a medium, dull, warm orange, we are more accurately describing the value, intensity, temperature and, thus, the hue.

Look what happens when we paint the same artichokes with slight shifts in temperature: warm (left) and cool (right).

TRADITIONAL COLOR SCHEMES

There are several traditional color schemes, each having color combinations that are either adjacent (neighboring colors on the color wheel) or contrasting (colors opposite one another on the color wheel). The most common color schemes are monochromatic, complementary, split complementary, analogous, and triadic. In addition to a combination of hues, a color scheme can also include tints, tones, shades, and altered intensities of those hues. Select one color from the scheme to dominate, either in value, intensity, detail, or area, or a combination thereof. Avoid using all the colors in the scheme at their full intensities unless you're aiming for a jarring effect, or trying to create a circus-like atmosphere.

The monochromatic color scheme includes variations on a single hue, in this case green.

The analogous color scheme includes any two to seven (if you count the intermediary mixtures each as two) adjacent colors on the color wheel. This sketch shows yellow, yellow-green, green-yellow, green, green-blue, blue-green, and blue.

The triadic color scheme includes three colors equidistant from one another—in this case, a subdued orange, violet in strongly contrasting values, and green (close in value to the orange).

The complementary color scheme includes two diametrically opposed colors (in this case red and green). Note that even though the green background in this sketch comprises a greater area than the pomegranate, it is of a lowered intensity, thus allowing the bright red of the pomegranate and its busy detail and value contrast to dominate.

The split complementary color scheme includes a key color and the two colors on either side of the key color's complement. The colors featured in here are yellow, red-violet, and blue-violet. In the iris, the most eye-catching color (because of intensity, temperature, and value contrasts) is the yellow, even though it's small in area. The green, though larger in area, blends in with the background and is thus less important.

Seeing Color Harmonies Around Us

Color schemes are everywhere we look. Unfortunately, we often don't see the trees for the forest. (No, that's not a malapropism.) We miss the details right in front of our eyes because we're caught up in the bigger picture. Let's take apart those "bigger pictures" and look for the details. We'll see that there are lovely color schemes in things from walls to rooftops, flowers to butterflies, skies to fields, threatening storms to delicate roses. We have only to look and really see!

When you're stuck for color scheme ideas, look through these pages. I have isolated many hues in each photograph.

These can be used in creating color schemes for painting anything from the subjects in this book, to landscapes, portraits, even abstract paintings. Not every hue in a selection need be used. (Often, the fewer we use, the better.) In fact, if you study the photographs, you will find additional hues that, due to space constraints, were omitted. You may even decide that a slight shift in intensity or value in a hue would suit you better.

Things to Consider

Ask yourself the following questions before deciding on a color scheme for your painting.

- What value do you want to be dominant (light, medium, dark)?
- Do you want a dark value composition on a light background or a light composition on a dark background?
- Do you want a strong or weak value contrast between the background and subject matter?
- What temperature do you want the dominant hue to be (warm or cool)?
- Do you want to use harmonious, similar hues or contrasting, complementary hues?
- What sort of intensity contrast do you want (weak, moderate, strong)?
- What mood do you want to create?

Imagine that you want to paint a bunch of bananas. Look through the photos in this section. You'll see several variations of yellow—from bright to creamy to low intensity to yellow-orange. Choose one of the yellows. Then imagine how you might use some of the other colors from the same photo to finish the painting. Try it again with hues from another photo. Can you picture a rendering of the bananas using the blues, beiges, and browns of this stormy sky picture? Too dull? You might want to brighten the dull yellow hue slightly. Let the colors in these pages inspire you but not limit your imagination.

As long as our vision is clear, our brain is bombarded continuously with color harmonies. All we have to do is remember to see. Some people listen without hearing. We must be careful that we don't miss the beauty of color because we look without seeing.

Thinking About Colors

Color choices can contribute to our paintings or detract from them. They guide the viewer to see what we want to be seen, or direct the viewer's eye elsewhere. They emphasize our subject matter, or call attention to themselves. They cause the viewer to linger longer, or send the viewer scurrying. They create a mood or a feeling, or just express, "Ho hum." And the scary thing is: The choice of colors and treatment is totally up to us. On the other hand, that's also the most exciting part of painting.

Using Color to Create a Mood

Colors have a profound effect on our emotions. Even if you have never painted, you already have some sense of color. See how easily you can conjure up colors to paint a circus scene, or a funeral. You get the idea. We readily associate some colors with certain circumstances, events, and emotions. Those color associations will, of course, be influenced not only by our individual and emotional preferences, but also by our cultural heritage. (For example, white is associated with mourning in China; in the United States, with weddings or purity.)

Make a list of some moods, sensations, and attributes, like aggressive, angry, comfortable, confused, delicate, energetic, fresh, happy, immature, innocent, melancholy, passionate, peaceful, pure, romantic, rustic, somber, tranquil, etc. What hues, values, and intensities do they suggest to you? Use this list later when you hit a creative block or are unsure what mood you would like your painting to reflect.

If you need to jumpstart your imagination for this exercise, look through a book of paintings—preferably one that spans many painting eras. Look with squinted eyes so you're less likely to be influenced by the subject matter. What feeling does the general color, value, and intensity of each painting engender? And which of these color applications are you most drawn to? Some of us prefer colors in strong opposition to one another, such as blue and yellow. Others find the strong opposition of colors jarring, and prefer more muted or grayed colors, or colors that lie closer to one another on the color wheel, or colors in fresher, cleaner, lighter tones. What do you like? Do you always like the same thing, or are there times when you're more drawn to something totally opposite?

Color Scheme Exercises

Of course, the best way to learn about painting color harmonies is to work with paint; but we needn't be limited to that one recourse. Listed below are several activities that will joggle the color cells in your brain. You will need, in addition to your painting supplies, a stack of old magazines, photographs, postcards, a sheet of clear acetate, scissors, and a package of colored construction paper—preferably one that has a wide range of colors, values, and intensities. From the package of construction paper, select one sheet of each value and intensity for every color. Cut the sheets in half crossways. Keep one set of half-sheets to represent different background colors. Use the other set to cut into shapes in the second exercise.

Choose a background color. When you need help selecting a background color for a painting, grab your paints and make color swatches—or a quick sketch—of your intended subject on the clear acetate. Hold the acetate against various colored papers. Pick the subject/background color combination that pleases you the most and that will support the effect you wish to accomplish. Keep in mind that you will probably need to adjust the hue, value, or intensity of that background color somewhat in the actual painting. Sometimes, a slight shift in value or intensity means the difference between a background color that supports your design and one that competes with it. Wipe the acetate clean to reuse.

Collect colors. Start a collection of travel and art postcards and photographs. Collect not only pictures with color schemes that please you but also ones that would cause you to broaden your taste for other color harmonies. You'll be surprised at how inspiring it can be to have a ready supply of color schemes.

Keep a notebook. Keep a looseleaf notebook in which you paste snips from magazines, ads, wallpapers, printed fabrics, wrapping papers, and so on. Or attach them to large poster boards. Try to analyze each entry to see what it is about that particular combination of colors that tickles your fancy. The more you analyze your reaction to the colors you see used together, the more at ease you'll become in creating your own color harmonies.

Take note. Buy a set of colored pencils and a small sketchbook. Carry them with you on trips across country, around the world, or just to the garden, local nursery, or museum. Make notes of interesting color combinations.

You will need:

- Craft clay or Play-Doh (clay should be a solid color)
- A light source (flashlight, desk lamp, table lamp, sunlight through a window)
- Toothpick or small twig
- Colored papers
- An orange and/or assorted objects and fruits
- A value scale (see page 29)

LIGHT AND SHADOW EXPERIMENTS

The mystery of light and shadow, and how they react with one another is a fascinating case, with clues scattered all around us. With just a few tools, we can solve the puzzle; and doing so will have a great impact on the effectiveness of our painting. To learn from this chapter, you're going to have to do some experiments. We learn best by doing.

Local Color, Shadows, and Highlights

Let's imagine, for a moment, that our clay is a new chunk of orange craft clay. We know that the piece of clay is the same color throughout—no variations, no light tints, no dark shades. The clay's color is called its *local color*. The following exercises will help you to see and understand local color as well as *highlight* (the area facing the light), *shadow* (the area facing away from the light), and *half-tones* (those subtle shifts in value between the highlight and shadow areas).

1. Roll the clay into a smooth, round ball, place it on a piece of paper, and shine a light on the upper right side. We know the entire ball is the same color throughout because we formed it ourselves from a single color clay. And yet, if we look carefully and compare, we can see that the ball is no longer that single, local color. The local color appears slightly washed out where the light hits it, and much darker where the light is absent. Look at the half-tone area—the area on which the light glances past at an angle rather than striking directly. Use your value scale to see how many values you can identify on the ball.
2. Now poke your finger in the top of the clay ball to make a depression. Set the ball back on the paper and beam the light across the top of it. What happens when the light shines across the depression? Which side of the depression is the highlight on? Which side is in shadow?
3. Next, push a toothpick or twig down in the depression, kind of like a stem.

4. Now, gather several solid-colored objects, any shape. Shine a light on each one separately. Look for the light and dark values and compare them with the local color. Use your value scale to try to determine the values of the local colors, the shadows, and the highlights.
5. Check the highlights against the pure white on your value scale. Are they a stark white? Try to determine whether the highlight colors are warm or cool.

Observe how the local color changes depending on where the light hits the orange.

Cast Shadows

We can further add to the three-dimensional perception by painting a cast shadow. *Cast shadows* are shadows caused by an object blocking the flow of light. Let's return to the clay ball and this time study the cast shadow.

1. Once again, shine the light on your clay ball. Notice the position and shape of the cast shadow. Move the light source around, raising it higher and lowering it. Place it directly above the ball.

2. Try the first experiment again, this time using a collection of other objects of various shapes. By paying attention to ordinary things in everyday life, we become more aware of cast shadows and how they're affected by the objects they fall across.

3. Rotate the paper on which your arrangement sits and observe the changes in the shapes of the shadows.

4. Set up your arrangement on a piece of white paper near a south facing window and check it periodically. Watch what happens to the shadows as the sun rises higher in the sky, or sinks, or fades.

5. Now let's look for even finer details. Select a few of your objects, and under the light, study the edges of the shadows. Move the light source closer and then farther away. When is the shadow's edge sharp? When is it more fuzzy? When is the shadow darkest? When is it faint?

6. Unless you're working in the dark with just a single light source, you will probably see other cast shadows, as well. See how many cast shadows you can find for a single object. What happens when two of those shadows overlap? Each shadow cast by a single object represents a different light source. See if you can identify which light source caused each shadow you see.

7. The cast shadow is affected by the color of the surface on which it falls. Place your object on different colored backgrounds. What happens to the color of the cast shadow? To more easily compare, let the object's shadow fall partially across two or three different colored pieces of paper at the same time.

8. The cast shadow is also affected by the color of the light that casts the shadow. Place an object on a piece of white paper near a south facing window. Make careful note of the color of the cast shadow in the cool light of early morning. Check on it again later in the afternoon when the light is warmer in color.

9. The next time you attend a performance where colored spotlights are used, notice the colors of the shadows that are cast. Security and streetlights will also cast different colored shadows. As you walk from one lighted area to another at night, watch the color of your shadow. In fact, try to become aware of the colors in every shadow you see.

10. Sometimes an intense light will cast a shadow the same color as the object, especially that part of the cast shadow that is closest to the object casting it. Try this: Outside, in bright sunlight, place an orange, an apple, and a lemon on a sheet of white paper. Arrange them so you can see each cast shadow separately. If your eyes aren't trained to notice subtle color variations, you may, at first, simply see a dark gray cast shadow. Look again. There are wonderful colors hiding in those shadows.

11. Place all the fruit on a piece of colored paper. Place the lemon slightly behind the apple. Shine a light on the apple, letting the shadow from the apple climb up onto the lemon. Notice how the shadow of the apple changes shape to wrap itself onto the contours of the lemon. And what color is the shadow cast onto the lemon?

Notice the beautiful colors in these cast shadows. For the orange, look for orange, red, and violet. For the apple, look for deep violet and blue.

Study the bottom edges of these fruits. Notice how light their color is from the yellow background reflected back up onto them.

Compare how much darker the lower edges of the fruits are now on the background. Study the transition of colors on the orange, from washed out color in the highlight area, to yellow, to yellow-orange, to orange, to red-orange, to red, and to violet along the lower edge.

Reflected Lights

Reflected lights are lights that are reflected off of nearby surfaces onto an object. The smoother, glossier, and shinier the nearby surfaces are the more likely they are to reflect light onto neighboring objects; a matte, dull surface would absorb much of the light. The reflected light is subtle—neither as strong nor as large as the true highlight area. It will be located adjacent to the surface reflecting it.

1. Place an orange on a yellow surface. Notice how the light that strikes the yellow surface bounces back up onto the orange's surface. That reflected light area will be a light yellow-orange, located near the edge of the orange, and close to the cast shadow. Your brain is telling you, "The orange is orange, and that's that." Experiment with different colors and with both shiny and matte surfaces until you find a combination that finally helps you see the reflected light. Once you begin to actually see a reflected light, it will become easier to recognize in the world around you.

2. On your yellow background, place a red apple, and a lime, or some other object near your orange. Can you see their colors reflected onto the adjacent surface of the orange? So now your orange has not only its local color, its washed out highlight color, its half tones, and its shadow colors, it has also colors of the surface on which it sits and colors of the objects surrounding it. But one of the wonderful things about objects being more than just a single local color is that we can use all those other colors to unify the subjects in our paintings. Reflected lights and cast shadows help us build connecting paths of color between the various subjects, thus helping the eye travel through the painting.

3. Now try a few white eggs on different colored backgrounds. See if you can identify the reflected lights using just the available light in your kitchen.

4. Put several white eggs on a white napkin, in a white bowl, on a white tablecloth. Look for all the colors hidden in all that white. For extra credit, after you have worked through several painting lessons, try to paint the eggs. You'll learn invaluable lessons while trying to capture the different whites in all their colors. Have fun!

This photo was shot in bright sunlight, resulting in a dark, hard-edged shadow.

This photo was taken a few moments later under an approaching cloud. Notice how the density of the shadow changes.

A few more moments later, and a lot more cloud. This soft edged, lighter value shadow illustrates how much the cloud had filtered the sunlight. Softer light, softer shadow.

The closer an object is to the surface on which its shadow falls, the closer it will be to touching that portion of its shadow. Notice that the sprouted leaves that touch the surface also touch the shadow. (Look for the bit of green reflected in the shadow where they touch.) The leaves that are farther away from the surface are also father away from their cast shadow.

Some Things to Remember

The list below will remind you of some of the things you should have discovered through your light and shadow experiments. If you haven't worked through the experiments yet, don't peek!

- A gentle light casts a fuzzy shadow.
- A bright light casts a dark shadow.
- A far light casts a soft shadow.
- A close light casts a hard shadow.
- A far light casts an elongated shadow. (Sunlight low on the horizon makes our personal shadow long, lean, and lanky.)
- A near light casts a condensed shadow. (Sunlight directly overhead makes our personal shadow short, squat, and stout.)
- Shadows are darkest near the object casting them.
- Shadows fade the farther they are from the object casting them.

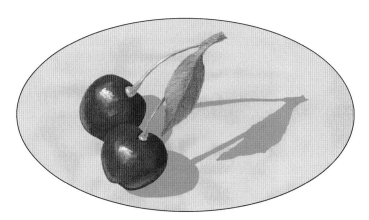

What kind of light casts a hard, long shadow like this?

Hints

- Walk around the arrangement to view it from different vantage points. Try removing and replacing objects while watching the adjacent surface to note subtle color changes. Try it under different lighting.
- To easily paint reflected lights and cast shadows, first slightly moisten the area to be painted with water or water plus an extender medium. Then sideload a flat brush (larger than you think you need) with color thinned with water and extender medium. Stroke the brush on the palette (over and over in the same spot) to blend the paint partially across the brush. Apply the stroke to the painting, using the water edge of the brush, if necessary, to soften any unwanted hard edges. Resist the temptation to keep fiddling with it. If your application appears too weak, dry the paint completely, then repeat the process. It's much better to apply too little paint than too much. You can easily build up depth of color with repeated layers, but you cannot as easily remove too heavy an application.
- Keep a strong flashlight or high intensity desk lamp handy at your painting table to experiment with lighting variations when you're painting from actual subject matter.

- Shadow colors are affected by: the object casting them; the surface color upon which they are cast; the objects surrounding them and reflecting light onto them.
- Some shadows may be cool; others, in the same arrangement, may be warm.
- The shadow's shape is affected by: the object casting the shadow; the shape of the object on which it falls; the proximity of the light; the angle of the light.
- Where light strikes, local color is washed out.
- Where no light strikes, local color is darkened.
- Where light is obstructed, a shadow is cast.
- Multiple light sources cast multiple shadows.
- When light passes across a depression, the highlight hits the far side of the depression; the shadow falls into the side of the depression nearest the light.
- Where multiple cast shadows overlap, the shadow will be darkest.
- Sometimes cast shadows will be the complementary color of the light causing the shadow.
- Light reflected by nearby objects onto a subject will affect the subject's local color.
- Highlights are rarely pure white. They may be warm or cool. To make a highlight seem stronger, contrast its temperature with that of the subject's local color. (For example, put a slightly greenish highlight on a red apple or a yellowish highlight on a purple grape.)
- To make a highlight seem lighter, paint the subject's local color darker.

COMPOSITION DESIGN FUNDAMENTALS

Just as knowing the letters of the alphabet enables us to build words, knowing the elements and principles of design and the effective placement of the focal area will help us build successful compositions. These fundamentals have long been recognized and used by artists, designers, and decorators.

Elements of Design

A design is made up of six elements: *line, shape, size, space, color, value, intensity, texture,* and *mass*. If you dissected even a child's crayon drawing, you would find these elements. In describing the elements, I have listed a few descriptive terms—sometimes of opposite extremes (light/dark, large/small, etc.). Not listed, but equally important, are all the variations between, and even beyond, the descriptions (very light, medium light, medium, medium dark, very dark, etc.). The descriptions are meant to inspire your thinking, not limit it to the few adjectives mentioned.

- **Line:** Straight or curved? Flowing and free or rigid and decisive? Horizontal (resting, tranquil), vertical (strong, rigid), or diagonal (activated, energized)? Blurry or bold? Delicate or sturdy? Actual or suggested (by something pointing, looking, or facing)?
- **Shape:** Free-form, rectangular, square, triangular, circular, oval, organic?
- **Size:** Large or small? This can pertain to the objects as well as the spaces or intervals between them.
- **Space:** Positive (occupied) or negative (empty)? Advancing or receding? Open or closed?
- **Color:** Warm (advancing) or cool (retreating)? Opaque or translucent? Harmonious, contrasting, or discordant combinations?
- **Value:** Light, cheerful, and delicate or dark, threatening, and somber?
- **Intensity:** Saturated (full strength, brilliant) or unsaturated (muted, grayed, subdued) color?
- **Texture:** Shiny like satin or nappy like velvet? Smooth or rough? Busy with detail or plain?
- **Mass:** Large or diminutive? Vigorous or delicate?

Focal Area

As we make our design selections based on the various elements, we also need to determine a focal area for our painting. A focal area attracts attention and then leads the viewer to continue looking. The focal area can be emphasized by, among other things, painting it with the strongest value and intensity contrasts, giving it the greatest detail and sharpest definition, and having lines within the composition direct attention to it.

We must be careful, however, not to be too ambitious, trying to make our entire painting full of focal points. When everything in the painting is a focal point, there is no focal point. Water droplets painted on every leaf and flower are useless and distracting unless we're painting a rainstorm. On the other hand, one or two droplets placed strategically on only the focal area will draw the viewer's attention directly to it.

And how do we decide where to position the focal area? First, we need to decide what type of balance we want in the composition: symmetrical (in which both sides of the painting appear almost as a mirror image, with the focal area placed along the center line); asymmetrical (in which the focal area is placed off center); radial (in which lines converge on or radiate from the center); or occult (in which there is no obvious focal area). Since the focal areas for the symmetrical and radial compositions rest on the center line, and there is no obvious focal area in the occult composition, let's focus our attention on asymmetrical balance.

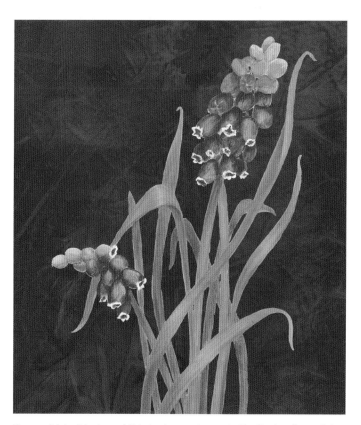

The marbleized texture of this background repeats the flowing lines of the grape hyacinth's strap-like leaves. The deep background color makes a striking contrast to the light flowers.

A quick and easy way to determine an ideal location for the focal area is to divide our painting surface into thirds, both horizontally and vertically. Any one of the four points at which the horizontal and vertical lines intersect would be an ideal location for a focal area. You will notice that any one point is located an unequal distance from the top and bottom of the illustrated rectangle and from the two sides. These same divisions can be applied to square or circular painting surfaces.

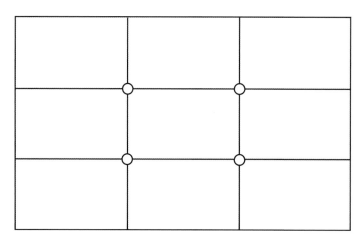

Choose one of the four intersecting points for the location of your focal area.

Principles of Design

The principles of design include dominance, contrast, rhythm and repetition, balance, transition, and unity. I have included a few thought-provoking questions or points with each principle, but, as with the elements, these questions or points are not meant to be all-inclusive. They are just to spur your thinking. Keep our hypothetical red rose (see sidebar at right) painting in mind as you read through these principles, and try to make some decisions relevant to how you might paint it.

Dominance

Dominance is that which first captures the viewer's attention. When designing a composition, ask yourself, for example, what will be the dominant . . .

- shape (horizontal, vertical, diagonal, circular, triangular)
- texture (smooth, rough, crisp, bristly, soft, stiff)
- color (warm or cool)
- intensity (subdued or brilliant)
- value (light or dark)
- line (curving or straight)

Contrast

Contrast is that which conflicts with the dominant shape, value, color, etc., thereby creating variety. A composition of all round fruits would be boring. Throw in a pineapple, all spiky and prickly, to create a bit of tension and excitement. Even something round and large among a collection of smaller round things helps break the monotony a little. An apple, especially one with a stem and leaves, placed among a composition of grapes, gooseberries, currants, and blueberries, adds variety of size and color, and its leaves and stem add some contrast in texture, shape, and line.

So, how shall we use contrast to make our hypothetical painting appealing, interesting, exciting? Here are some ideas:

- Cool colors in a warm painting? (With our red rose, red flowers, and red ribbon, something a little cooler in color would certainly offer variety and relief.)
- Straight lines among curved ones? (Rose petals are softly curved, likewise the flow of the leaves and the ribbon. Thorny,

A Hypothetical Painting

Let's imagine that we'd like to paint a composition in warm colors, consisting of a red rose, other predominantly red flowers, a vase, a red ribbon, and maybe an ornate figurine. Let's say the rose is to be our main attraction. Where, within the focal areas, shall we place the rose? With all that competing red, how can we ensure that the rose will be the main attraction? We might set the rose apart by making it a larger, more dominating size; surrounding it with complementary green leaves; using stronger value contrasts within the rose; or subduing the intensities of the other red flowers and the red ribbon to prevent the eye from wandering aimlessly.

We could further ensure that the rose will grab attention by arranging lines, shapes, or colors to lead the eye to it. We could take the rose out of the vase and place it slightly apart. An isolated item will draw the eye, particularly if we also set it off with strong value contrasts. We can guide the viewer through our painting by the thoughtful use of the principles of design, which will help us make all the "lots of little decisions" we need to consider.

stiff rose stems, if not totally obscured by the other flowers and leaves, would provide some sturdy, straight lines. Otherwise, perhaps our choice of other accompanying flowers, vase, or background treatment could provide the needed contrast.)

- Lines curving in an opposite direction from the dominant lines?
- Bug-eaten flowers or leaves among otherwise perfect ones?
- Busy, precise details or patterns in an otherwise calm painting?
- Lost or softened edges in a sharply focused painting?
- A dark value in a predominantly light painting?
- A complementary color (green leaves) added to a predominantly harmonious color theme (various reds)?
- Contrasting sizes (our large rose among smaller roses and red flowers)?
- Horizontal elements in a vertical theme (a drape across the table or a horizontal figurine)?
- A geometric form (our vase, perhaps) in a composition of irregular, organic shapes?

Rhythm and Repetition

Rhythm and *repetition* keep the viewer's eye moving through the painting. Be cautious about repeating identical shapes, sizes, colors, and intervals. Such repetition can seem static and boring. Three identical flowers in a line, evenly spaced apart, are predictable and unexciting. Change the spacing between them, putting two closer together. Or bring one of the groupings of two closer to the foreground. Or change the sizes. Or tip one flower in a different direction. We will still keep the viewer's eye moving through repetition from one flower to the next in the overall composition, but the trip will be more interesting.

Balance

Balance refers to that combination of elements that creates visual stability in the painting. From birth, we have an innate sense of balance. As a newborn, our perception of impending loss of balance caused a great flailing of arms and legs. Then came the struggle to oppose gravity and balance muscles against one another. As adults, we continue to find a lack of balance distressing, whether it is a physical situation or a visual one. So we want to be sure we create a comfortable balance in our paintings. Too much weight on one side of a painting will make it appear unbalanced. When we place our focal area on the spot we identified earlier, we must balance it with what we do to the other side of the painting. Keep the following tips in mind:

- A small, intense colored area can balance a larger area of subdued color.
- A small area of visual texture or more detail can balance a larger, smoother, less busy area.

- A small area of sharply contrasting value can balance a larger area of mildly contrasting value.
- A small area of warm color can balance a larger area of cool color.
- A small mass near the edge of the painting can balance a larger mass near the center (seesaw).
- A single angular shape can balance a bunch of circles or ovals.
- A small complex shape can balance a larger, simpler shape.

Transition

Transition (sometimes called *gradation*) is that which relates one element to the next, such as the way white on the value scale is related to black by the intervening shades of gray. Transition can be created by the way we use color, value, line, space, texture, and so forth to move the eye through the painting. Imagine a painting made only of colors as they came from the tubes or bottles. The sky would be one shade of blue; the grass, one green; the tree trunks, one brown. With no intermixing, there would be no smooth transition from the tree to the sky or the grass, no transitional color to carry the eye easily from one form to the next. Instead, the jump from brown trunk to green grass or blue sky would be sudden and uncontrolled. We may not end up looking where the artist wanted us to look. Whereas mixing a transitional color by

The light pepper amidst so much darkness draws our eye instantly. A second or third yellow pepper added to the group would dilute the impact. If we had hoped to have the purple pepper be the focal point, thinking its unique shape and color, and the fact that we had placed it in front would set it apart from the others, we would have been disappointed. Even a dozen purple peppers could not equal the eye-catching power of the contrasting single yellow pepper.

adding a little of the blue from the sky into part of the tree trunk and limbs would provide a visual bridge from the tree to the sky. Directing the line of the tree branch to point to or overlap the roof line of a house would provide transition from the line of the tree and carry the eye along from tree to house. Following are some things we can consider to provide transition in our paintings:

- Use color through reflected lights to tie neighboring forms together.
- Use the dark values of shadows to lead the eye from one place to the next.
- Use gradually changing values, colors, lines, shapes, sizes, and spaces to relate one area to the next.
- Bend a branch, curve a drape, fold over a leaf, or angle a prop to lead the eye to the next element or contour.
- Overlap elements to provide transition.

Unity

Unity (sometimes called *harmony*) is that combination or arrangement of all the elements of the painting to make everything appear to belong together. Through clever use of the elements and principles you could even make a lobster and an Easter basket appear to belong together.

For a painting to have unity does not mean that it should be overwhelmed with "sameness." If, in fact, there is too much sameness or equality, then there is no unity or harmony because our attention is equally divided. Variety makes a painting interesting. Variety can be achieved by making adjustments in sizes, values, color, shapes and so on, and still create harmony or unity. Every aspect of the painting must work together and share the load of making the painting a success.

Using yellow's complementary color, violet, to shade the squash anchors the squash to the mottled violet background by providing a transition. Touches of yellow in the background help connect the yellow squash to it. The arrangement of the squashes creates stability in balance; and the warty versus smooth skin provides contrast.

BACKGROUND COLORS

Consider what happens to the different subjects in these sketches with each change of background color. To make it easier for you to compare the effect backgrounds can have, I have kept many of the subject colors fairly identical in each sketch. As such, most of the subjects are not well unified with the backgrounds. Compare what happens, however, when the background color is introduced into the subjects (see the artichokes on the red, dark green, and purple backgrounds). Try to determine what works, what does not, and what you'd do differently. Think of ways you might change the values and intensities of the subjects and/or the backgrounds to more prominently feature or subdue particular subjects.

Unifying Subject and Background

Our backgrounds are most effective when their colors work in conjunction with the subject matter they surround. After you have chosen the color, value, and intensity for the subject matter and background of your painting, you have to make sure that the two work together. There are a number of ways in which you can unify the subject matter of the painting with the background.

- Mix a little of the background color into the colors used for painting the subject. This will also lower the intensity of the subject colors.
- Use the background color to shade or highlight the subject, depending upon the color.

- Let the background color peek through the subject matter. You will notice when you work through the step-by-step lessons that this is a technique I use a lot. Depending upon the hue and value of my background, I may let it help suggest the shading, the highlighting, or the general color of my subject by applying the subject's local coloring thinly over the background.

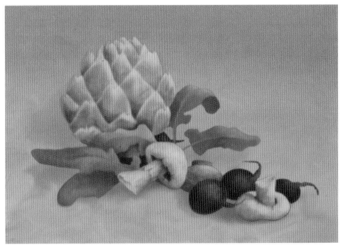

Just as we nearly lost the radishes on the red, we barely see—at first glance—the mushrooms on the tan. Without the dark contrast inside the caps, and the surrounding radishes, they would really be lost. To preserve the mushrooms, we could change their hue slightly, or change the value that surrounds them. To focus more attention on the artichoke and less on the radishes, we could deepen the shading and details on the artichoke and soften the colors and contrasts of the radishes.

The low-intensity red of the background, because it is the complementary color of green, sets off the greens nicely. The contrast pulls our gaze to the artichoke and the leaves. Ah, but which will we focus on—artichoke or leaves? The size and busy detail of the artichoke help it take center stage. Those curved, pointed petals and all the detail in the scars scream, "Look at me!" The value contrast (light versus dark) pulls our eye from one mushroom to the next. The radishes are melting right into the background. To keep them from disappearing entirely, we could darken the red behind them and/or brighten (change the intensity of) and lighten (change the value of) their hue slightly.

On the light green background, we lose a major part of our composition, but we certainly found the radishes! If we absolutely wanted a green background, would it help to darken its value? You bet! We would regain somewhat the "lost" portion of the composition—the artichoke and the leaves. The strong value contrast of a darker green background would also throw the spotlight on the very light mushrooms.

On this light green background, look what happens when we adjust the hue, value, and intensity of the radishes. They "fit" better with the rest of the subject matter, giving a soft, gentle effect. And, in spite of the fact that I've even added a fifth radish, the radishes don't command attention as they do on the light green background at left.

On the dark green background, the leaves are unobtrusive, focusing attention on the other subjects. The mushrooms first catch our eye, particularly the long-stemmed one, because of the strong value contrast and detail. From there, our eye is pulled upward to the artichoke, lured by the bright, light contrast, and by the upward thrust of the artichoke leaves. Now, perhaps, we notice the radish leaves and follow the downward curves to settle on the radishes. Having touches of red scumbled throughout the background helps balance the red of the radishes, making them not so unique a color.

This violet background seems a little too sweet for these hearty veggies. And there's no unity between the subject and the background, even though I added violet tones in all the items. Could we make a violet background work? Possibly. One way would be to lower both the intensity and the value of the background to create a more earthy tone. Then we'd need to adjust all the colors in the sketch, working more violet into the mixtures. That would help anchor the composition. If we wanted to showcase the mushrooms, we could tint them a warm gold (yellow being the complement of violet). Touches of golden highlights on the artichoke and leaves would help the eye travel through the composition.

SURFACE PREP AND FAUX FINISHES

You can re-create the backgrounds I used in the step-by-step lessons with a few additional supplies. Or you can use the tools and techniques discussed here to create your own backgrounds. The photos on the next three pages illustrate some special backgrounds and faux finishes I used in the lessons.

Brushes for Basecoating

For general basecoating, I use a Loew-Cornell Series 7550 ¾- or 1-inch flat brush. Although the brushes are expensive, they are worth the investment over time. Well cared for, they will last for years, and will outperform dozens of foam brushes, facilitating the application of smooth basecoats and finishes and crisp, sharp edges for trimming. For special effects such as scumbling (stroking several colors in an overlapping crisscross fashion), I use the 1-inch brush of that series. To paint streaks, I like a 1-inch chip brush.

Several of the backgrounds call for the application of thin washes of color. When applying washes for marbleizing or other texturizing techniques, you may find it helpful to work with extender or retarding mediums and water mixed in your paints. This will give you more working time before the paint starts to set up. And of course, the larger the brush you use, the more quickly you will be able to work. When you do add mediums to your paint, be sure to dry the wash thoroughly with a hair dryer before proceeding to the next step. Otherwise, the thinned layer may lift off when wetted with the next paint application.

Apply thinned paint with a stiff-bristled brush to create a streaky bakground.

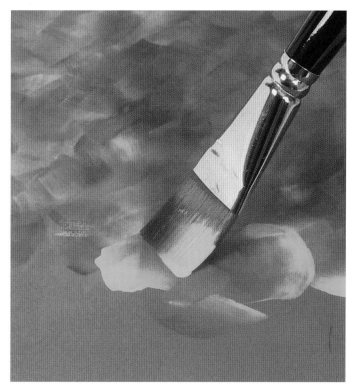

Scumble strokes in a crisscross fashion to create a broken-color background.

Create a crackled, aged appearance with a weathered wood finishing product.

Using a Mini Paint Roller

For painting some backgrounds on large surfaces, a 2-inch mini paint roller is convenient. To paint a gradated wash over a solid background color, first apply a thin layer of water plus painting medium with the roller. Then, with the water and medium remaining in the roller, pick up the desired color and roll it on the area you wish to be the darkest value. As you work away from the starting point, you will have less and less paint in the roller and the color will be fainter.

To achieve a more opaque coverage with gradated colors, begin with the lighter value color. Starting at one end of your painting surface, roll the color on, covering about one fourth to one third of the area. Then doubleload the roller with the light color on one edge and the next color on the other edge. Roll those two on, slightly overlapping the previous application with the light edge of the roller, and working to create a smooth blend. To add another color or value, roll as much of the light value off the roller onto paper towels as you can. Then, again, doubleload the roller, this time with the new color and the one just previously used. Be careful not to pick up the roller from one area of the painting and jump to another area—you'll get a sudden shift of colors or values. Instead, roll from one area to another, letting the colors blend as you go. Consider basecoating the surface first with a color that would enhance the effect you're hoping to create, a color that would help pull together any colors you're going to roll on top of it.

Special Effects

Household sponges, sea sponges, chamois cloth, and crumpled plastic wrap pressed into wet paint to lift it off, or filled with paint to press it onto a surface, result in some interesting effects. Sponges and chamois cloth leave a soft-edged effect, especially when working with thinned paint. Plastic wrap imparts crisper details. Use sponges, chamois cloth, and plastic wrap to create leather-, granite-, and marble-like effects.

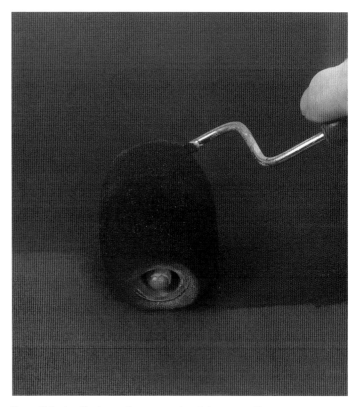

Use a 2-inch roller to easily merge colors into one another, for a gradated background.

Drybrush across raised streaks of dry paint to leave slight glints of color.

Press crumpled plastic wrap, chamois cloth, or a sponge into wet paint to create a leather-like texture.

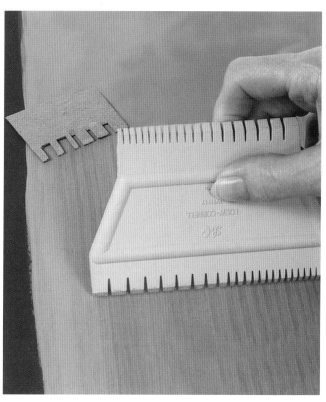

To create a background that resembles wood, streak the paint with a woodgraining comb or a piece of cardboard with "teeth" cut in it.

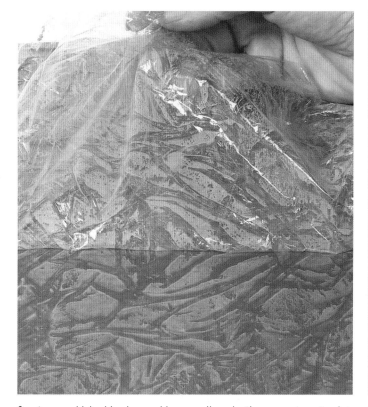

Create a marbleized background by spreading plastic wrap onto wet paint.

Roll paint across a plastic onion bag for a unique texture.

APPLES

Apples conjure up all kinds of rustic, down-home associations. After all, what is more American than Mom's apple pie? An orchard is the perfect scene of tranquility, with the wonderful textures of the trees and leaves and the perfect springtime freshness of the blossoms. Apples, with their bold shape and color, add strength to any picture. And, polished to a high gloss, they provide a perfect highlight.

PALETTE
- Titanium White
- Yellow Light
- Cadmium Yellow
- Antique Gold
- Terra Coral
- Light Avocado
- Wild Orchid
- Banana Cream
- Evergreen

BRUSHES
- Flats: Nos. 4, 8, and 10
- Liner: No. 1

Hints

1. Use the No. 10 flat brush to paint the apple, the Nos. 4 and 8 flat brushes to paint the leaves, and the No. 4 flat brush and the No. 1 liner brush to paint the stems. If you have an old, splayed bristle (hair) liner brush, use it to dab on the freckles in step 4.
2. Let's make these apples really glow. Begin with a white undercoat followed by a bright yellow wash. If you prefer a more subtle yellow, simply choose a more subdued undercoat, such as Moon Yellow (see a sample of that color on the bananas worksheet on page 54).

3. Notice how a dark, busy background, such as the one on the worksheet, calls for the more opaque coverage provided by a white undercoat. If you're working on a plain, light background you can skip the white undercoat.
4. In step 1, I show you two yellow options. I like the glow of the lighter yellow through the slightly more orange yellow. If you prefer a brighter apple, apply two coats of the bright yellow and omit the darker one.
5. Refer to all colors on the lesson page to match and mix colors.

Contour Lines

To help you sense the three dimensionality of the apple (and other rounded subjects), draw contour lines on the pattern, starting at the center base of the apple and pulling upward into the stem depression. Continue adding lines to each side, curving slightly outward. Notice how the tops and bottoms of the strokes curve toward the straight center line in the front, and away from it in the back. Also notice how that straight center line tilts with the axis of the apple. The apple in step 5 is more tilted than the one in step 4, so the color placement tilts accordingly.

1. Apples: Undercoat with Titanium White (see hints 2 and 3). Allow to dry. Cover with Yellow Light; dry; then apply a coat of Cadmium Yellow. Leaves: Undercoat with Light Avocado.

2. Apples: Add shading with a sideloaded wash of Antique Gold. Leaves: Add sideloaded accents of Terra Coral and Wild Orchid.

3. Apples: Paint a sideloaded accent of Terra Coral. Add sideloaded Light Avocado in the stem depression and to deepen the shadow. Leaves: Shade with a sideload of Evergreen. Highlight with a sideload of Cadmium Yellow + Light Avocado + Evergreen.

4. Apples: Repeat step 3 using Wild Orchid very thinly in the shadow area. Dab on thin Yellow Light plus very little Wild Orchid for the freckles. Drybrush Banana Cream in the highlight area. Add a reflected light of sideloaded Yellow Light. Leaves: Add veins with very thin Light Avocado + Yellow Light + Evergreen.

5. Stems: Mix Light Avocado + Terra Coral + Antique Gold to undercoat. Shade with Evergreen + Terra Coral. Highlight with Antique Gold. Apples: Cover the apple with a wash of Cadmium Yellow to pull all the colors together. Dry. Add a strong highlight of Banana Cream within the highlight area. Holes in leaves: Outline with the dark stem mixture. Fill in with the color you would see through the hole.

Apples Reference Photos

Fortunately for us painters, there are thousands of varieties
of apples, giving us a wide range of colors, sizes, and shapes
from which to choose subjects for our paintings. Apples can
be elongated, round, angular, streaked, freckled, and more.
For creating paintings, we can also draw great inspiration
from the variety of uses for apples: for eating; for making jelly,
preserves, pies, and desserts; for juice and cider;
and for keeping the doctor away!

Bananas

By including a partially peeled banana in a painting, we can create the illusion of interrupted activity—thus adding interest to the painting, and possibly creating anticipation or curiosity in the viewer. Plus, the soft texture of the inner skin provides a pleasing contrast, especially if there are other unpeeled bananas in the painting.

PALETTE
- Moon Yellow
- Sand
- Antique White
- Raw Umber
- Forest Green
- Dioxazine Purple
- Pineapple
- French Grey Blue
- Sable Brown
- Marigold

BRUSHES
- Flats: Nos. 6 and 8
- Liner: No. 10/0

Hints

1. Use the largest flat brush you can handle for all work except the details in steps 2 and 5. Use the liner brush for the details.
2. Apply shading colors in very thin washes to build up the depth of shading gradually. It's easy to make shading darker with successive thin coats; it's much more difficult to lighten too heavy an application. Allow paint to dry thoroughly between applications.
3. If you're not fond of the bold, contrasting colors (blue and yellow) used on the worksheet, try some other combinations, such as the ones shown at right.
4. Refer to all colors on the lesson page to match and mix colors.

Notice how I've carried the background colors into the bananas. This makes a bridge from the subject to the background—or, in other cases, to the neighboring object—offering the eye some areas of smooth transition from one color to another.

1. Undercoat the banana peels with Moon Yellow. Undercoat the fruit with Sand and the inside of the peel with Antique White + Sand.

2. Shade the inside of the peel with Antique White + Raw Umber. Use the liner brush and Antique White + Raw Umber to paint thin lines on the fruit. Shade the peels with Moon Yellow + Dioxazine Purple. Tinge the tips of the banana peels with a sideloaded wash of Forest Green.

3. Scumble touches of Pineapple on the peel. Shade the peel with a sideloaded wash of French Grey Blue.

4. Shade the fruit first with Antique White, then with Sable Brown. Intensify the shading on the inside of the peel with Sable Brown. Scumble a thin wash of Marigold over the peels.

5. Use the liner brush to paint the edges of the open peel with Moon Yellow + Marigold. Intensify the shading on the fruit and the inside of the peel, and add blemishes on the peels with scant amounts of Raw Umber.

Bananas Reference Photos

The bright, happy yellow color and long curving shapes of bananas can add a pleasing accent to our paintings. Their geometry also allows us to pose them in many ways to complement an arrangement. Study the effects light and shadow have on the various planes. A loosened banana peel adds an element of casualness. Peel a banana and look closely for the subtle color variations between the fruit of the banana and the inside of the peel.

BELL PEPPERS

Bell (or sweet) peppers are available in a variety of colors. After you paint the yellow, green, and red ones in this lesson, try painting orange and purple ones. Work with the actual produce in front of you to help determine the colors you'll need for each step.

YELLOW PEPPERS PALETTE
- Moon Yellow
- Cadmium Yellow
- Pineapple
- Orchid
- Terra Coral

GREEN PEPPERS PALETTE
- Olive Green
- Forest Green
- Mistletoe
- Pineapple
- Terra Coral

RED PEPPERS PALETTE
- Cadmium Red
- Napa Red
- Terra Coral
- Pineapple

BRUSHES
- Flats: Nos. 2 and 8
- Liner: No. 10/0

Hints

1. Use the No. 8 flat brush to paint the peppers, the No. 2 flat brush to paint the stems, and the liner brush to add details to the stems.
2. You'll note that I've rearranged the step-by-step procedure a bit for each color variety. This is just to show you that the hues and values are more important than the sequence of steps in most cases. You might find that it's easier for you to visualize shapes within the pepper (or any subject) by first establishing the dark areas as shown in the first part of step 2 of the red peppers. Or if you relate better by identifying the lightest areas (as in the first part of step 2 of the green peppers), then put them in first. Or, maybe it's more helpful to you to apply the overall wash color first (as in the first part of step 2 of the yellow peppers) so you have it to compare lights and darks against.
3. Take a moment to study steps 3 and 4 for the yellow peppers.

Notice that I chose to shade the pepper with violet (the complementary color of yellow). This is a more colorful way to create shading colors than mixing a dark brown or black with the local color to darken it. And rather than mixing the complementary color with the local color, I like to paint with it directly, then submerge it with a thin wash layer of the local color.

4. Notice also in step 4, the reddish glow of the reflected light. You can see it most readily in the yellow peppers (review Reflected Lights on page 39).
5. Refer to all colors on the lesson page to match and mix colors.

Painting the Stems

(Use the color palette for the green peppers.)

1. Use the flat brush to undercoat the stem with Olive Green. Dab a mixture of Mistletoe + Terra Coral + Pineapple on the cut end.
2. Cover the stem with a thin wash of Mistletoe.
3. Use the liner brush to streak the stem with Forest Green.
4. Shade the stem with a sideload of Forest Green.

Yellow Peppers Palette

Green Peppers Palette

Red Peppers Palette

Yellow Peppers

1. Undercoat with Moon Yellow.

2. Apply a thin wash of Cadmium Yellow. Then highlight with a sideload of Pineapple.

3. Shade with a sideload of Orchid.

4. Apply a thin wash of Cadmium Yellow over the shading to submerge it into the pepper. Dry thoroughly before adding a reflected light with thinned Terra Coral sideloaded on the brush.

Green Peppers

1. Undercoat with Olive Green.

2. Highlight with a sideload of Pineapple. Shade with a sideload of Forest Green.

3. Apply a thin wash of Mistletoe over the entire pepper. Strengthen the highlight with Pineapple.

4. Strengthen the shading with Terra Coral + Forest Green. Add additional touches of Terra Coral.

Red Peppers

1. Undercoat with Cadmium Red.

2. Shade with a sideload of Napa Red. Dry. Then apply a wash of thinned Napa Red over the entire pepper. While the wash is wet, wipe out highlight areas with a clean, damp brush.

3. Highlight with a sideload of Terra Coral.

4. Accentuate the highlights with Pineapple. Paint the reflected light along the lower edge of the pepper with a sideload of Terra Coral.

Bell Peppers Reference Photos

Look closely at the lineup of multicolored peppers. Notice how many highlights appear on a single pepper—one for every lump and bump facing the light source. A cut pepper, showing its seed mass and ribs, adds a fascinating, busy bit of detail, and a welcome contrast from all the slickness of the almost plastic-looking peppers.

CARROTS

If you've ever plucked a carrot from the earth, rinsed it under a hose, and tasted its just-picked freshness, you can appreciate how a painting of carrots with their fresh, green tops could evoke memories of that crunchy, sweet, wholesome taste.

PALETTE
- Pumpkin
- Tangerine
- Burnt Orange
- Burgundy Wine
- Prussian Blue
- Banana Cream
- Avocado
- Mistletoe

BRUSHES
- Flat: No. 8
- Liner: No. 10/0

Hints

1. Use the flat brush to paint the carrots, fronds, and stems. Use the liner brush to paint the fine hair roots.

2. For best results in painting the carrots' delicate fern-like fronds, use the chisel edge of the flat brush. Load a thinned mixture of Avocado + Prussian Blue + Burgundy Wine into the brush and paint clusters with tapping/dabbing strokes. Repeat at least a second and a third time, each time using a lighter value and slightly thicker paint.

3. To paint the stems, use the same color mixtures as for the fronds. Holding the flat brush perpendicular to the surface, slide on the chisel edge, laying down thin streaks of color. By using the flat brush, rather than a liner brush, the delineation between your values will be softer and more natural looking.

4. Refer to all colors on the lesson page to match and mix colors.

If the complementary color scheme of the worksheet sketch is too bold for your tastes, try a more harmonious combination with this analogous scheme.

Tops and Stems

1. Dab thinned Avocado + Prussian Blue + Burgundy Wine.

2. Dab thinned Avocado.

3. Dab thinned Avocado and Mistletoe + Banana Cream.

Carrots

1. Undercoat carrots with Pumpkin.

2. Highlight with Tangerine, leaving spaces to suggest indentations.

3. Apply a wash of Burnt Orange over the whole carrot. Dry completely. Then shade edges and indentations with Burnt Orange sideloaded on the brush.

4. Intensify shading with a sideloaded wash of Burnt Orange + Burgundy Wine + Prussian Blue.

5. Accent highlights by drybrushing a mixture of Pumpkin + Banana Cream. Use the liner brush to paint hair-like roots with Pumpkin.

6. Deepen shading and add shadows with a sideloaded wash of Prussian Blue.

Carrots Reference Photos

Carrots' strong, readily identifiable color and shape lend a comfortable sense of familiarity to a painting. Their long, flowing, fern-like tops add a softness to hard edges and a sense of freshness. Notice the fine hair-like roots on the carrot and the creases girdling its circumference.

CHERRIES

Cherries are available in a great number of shapes and colors. As small fruits, they are handy to use for filling in areas in your painting, or to scatter as needed to help repeat colors in different areas. Clusters can be used for hanging or draping.

PALETTE
- Deep Blush
- Terra Coral
- Naphthol Red
- Napa Red
- Cranberry Wine
- Banana Cream
- Desert Turquoise
- Celery Green
- Light Avocado
- Evergreen
- Yellow Green

BRUSHES
- Flats: Nos. 4, 6, and 8
- Liner: No. 1

Hints

1. Use the No. 8 flat brush to paint the leaves, the No. 6 flat brush for the cherries, and the liner brush for the leaf veins and to basecoat the stems.

2. To paint lateral veins on both sides of the leaves, sideload the No. 8 flat brush (use the No. 4 on the smallest leaves) with very thin Evergreen. Begin at the base of the leaf with the color side of the brush facing toward the leaf tip. Paint a gentle, curving stroke, in the shape of a stretched out S, from the center vein toward the margin of the leaf. Immediately make the next stroke, allowing the water side of the brush to overlap slightly onto the previous stroke and soften it.

3. To paint the underside of the leaf, paint through step 3. Then delineate the veins with the liner and Yellow Green + Banana Cream. Next, sideload the No. 8 flat brush with Evergreen. Holding the paint side of the brush facing the center vein, paint an inverted V shape to tuck into the space between the lateral veins, thus shading between the veins. Allow to dry. Then brush over the leaf with Yellow Green or Evergreen + Yellow Green. Dry. Drybrush the leaf with Banana Cream.

4. Refer to all colors on the lesson page to match and mix colors.

Emphasize lateral veins with sideloaded, inverted V-shaped marks.

To paint the leaf without a turned edge, use the dotted line on this pattern.

Branch
Undercoat with Celery Green + Napa Red. Shade with Evergreen + Napa Red.

a

1. Cherries: (a) Undercoat with Deep Blush. Dry. (b) Then apply a wash of Terra Coral. Stems: (a) Basecoat with Celery Green. (b) Shade with Light Avocado. Leaves: Undercoat with Celery Green.

b

2. Cherries: (a) Apply a wash of Naphthol Red, letting it fade as it nears the highlight area. Allow to dry. (b) Then apply a shading wash of Napa Red. Stems: Shade deeper by sliding along the length of the stem with a sideload of thin Evergreen on the flat brush. Leaves: Apply a loose wash of Yellow Green on the left of the leaf and Light Avocado on the right.

a

b

3. Cherries: (a) Deepen the shading with a sideload of Cranberry Wine. Allow to dry. (b) Merge colors together with a thin sideload of Naphthol Red and/or Terra Coral. Stems: Add touches of sideloaded Naphthol Red or Napa Red to further shade the stems. Leaves: Add veins with a sideload of thin Evergreen (see hint 2).

To paint the underside of a leaf, see hint 3.

a

b

4. Cherries: (a) Paint highlights and reflected lights with a sideload of thinned Banana Cream. Blend out the edges. (b) Add a stronger highlight in the center of the highlight area with Banana Cream. Apply a sideloaded wash of reflected light color. On these cherries, I used Desert Turquoise. On the grouping above, I used Naphthol Red. Stems: Add a highlight of Banana Cream. Dry. Then cover the stems with thin Yellow Green. Leaves: Intensify colors by adding additional washes of Evergreen and Yellow Green. Try some Evergreen over Yellow Green, and some Yellow Green over Evergreen.

a

b

Cherries Reference Photos

Cherries come in a wide variety of shapes and colors. Notice the bowl of cherries, which shows different varieties, as well as a good contrast of darks and lights.

CORN

I focused this lesson on painting dried Indian corn as it provides an opportunity to play with a large variety of color washes. To paint fresh sweet corn, two sideloaded crescent strokes of deep yellow per kernel will do the trick.

Hints

PALETTE
- Sand
- Light Buttermilk
- Yellow Ochre
- Raw Sienna
- Raw Umber
- Heritage Brick
- Black Plum
- Plum
- Cranberry Wine
- Cadmium Yellow
- Honey Brown
- Russet
- Deep Burgundy
- Khaki Tan
- Banana Cream

BRUSHES
- Flats: Nos. 2 and 6
- Liner: No. 10/0
- Old toothbrush

1. Use the No. 6 flat brush to paint the corn and husks, the No. 2 flat brush to color the kernels and paint the nail and twine, and the liner to paint the silks.
2. The trick to painting Indian corn is to apply the sideloaded, thinned colors for the individual kernels—over a solid undercoat—with a small flat brush.
   - For each kernel, paint two crescent strokes around the outside edges, leaving the inner section as a highlight area.
   - In step 11, to intensify the highlights, dab them on with the corner of the No. 2 flat brush. The flat brush will create a soft, realistic, random effect.
   - An optional wash of color after step 11 will totally change the appearance. Step 12 illustrates a wash of Cranberry Wine; however, other colors would also work.
3. To undercoat the husks, hold the flat brush upright and slide on the chisel edge, laying the paint down in ridges (to create texture and variety) as it is forced out of the brush hairs.
   - Follow the contours of the husk. Add a few lighter veins with the liner brush and thick paint. The wash color, applied in step 3, will settle among the ridges, creating variety in color and value.
   - To apply shading (steps 4, 5, and 6), sideload the flat brush with thinned paint. Hold the brush perpendicular to the surface and slide lightly on the chisel edge, pushing the paint back and forth following the contours to suggest veins. For broader, deeper shaded areas, work with the brush held at a 45-degree angle and paint from the flat side.

4. To paint fresh, green husks, substitute greens for the colors used in painting the dried husks in steps 3 to 6. Keep the inner husks lighter in value.
5. Refer to all colors on the lesson page to match and mix colors.

Indian Corn

1. Undercoat the husks with the flat brush and Sand (see hint 3).
2. Use the liner brush to paint the veins with Light Buttermilk. Dry thoroughly.
3. Apply a thin wash of Yellow Ochre with the flat brush.
4. Apply shading with a sideload of thinned Raw Sienna on the flat brush.
5. Deepen shading with a sideload of thinned Raw Umber.

Paint the nail Raw Umber. Paint the twine streaks of Heritage Brick, Cranberry Wine, and Yellow Ochre.

6. Add touches of thinned Plum, Cranberry Wine, or Deep Burgundy.

7. Use an old, stiff brush to spatter husks with thinned Raw Umber.

8. Undercoat the corn with Yellow Ochre on the flat brush.

9. Use a pencil to draw kernels.

10. Sideload the flat brush with color and paint two crescent strokes per kernel. Shown here are kernels of Heritage Brick, Black Plum, Plum, Cranberry Wine, Cadmium Yellow, Honey Brown, Russet, Deep Burgundy, and Khaki Tan.

11. Highlight kernels with thinned Banana Cream.

12. To adjust the color of the entire ear, apply a thin wash of color (Cranberry Wine is shown).

Paint corn silks Raw Umber.

Sweet Corn

Undercoat with Banana Cream. Shade with Cadmium Yellow plus a tad of Deep Burgundy. Highlight with Light Buttermilk. Highlight again, if needed, with pure white.

Corn Reference Photos

Corn, with its tall, tasseled stalks, looks more impressive in the field than perhaps any other vegetable. Half shucked, it is still impressive with its silky hairs and splayed, multi-layered husk. A partially shucked ear of corn in a painting would seem to suggest temporarily interrupted activity, giving the painting a feel of the immediate present. The husk, ranging from fresh-picked green to papery, dry brown, is adaptable to many color schemes. Try painting the partially shucked, fresh ear pictured as if it were Indian corn. Make the silks dry, crinkly, and brown; and match`the coloring in the husks to the dried ones shown.

GARLIC

Garlic bulbs have lots of character, making them fun to paint. Line up a half dozen and they'll all be quite different. The torn bits of crinkly outer skin, the center stalk, the mass of curly roots, and the knobby lumps of the individual cloves all make garlic an interesting candidate for a painting.

Hints

PALETTE
- Buttermilk
- Sand
- Khaki Tan
- Light Buttermilk
- Raw Umber
- Black Plum
- French Mauve

BRUSHES
- Flats: Nos. 6 and 8
- Liner: No. 10/0

1. Use the No. 8 flat brush to paint the whole garlics, the No. 6 flat brush to paint the cloves, and the liner brush to paint the veins, broken skin details, and the roots.
2. Garlic can spice up a vegetable design as delightfully as it spices up a meal. Place some fresh garlic nearby to study as you paint. You might be surprised at the variety of subtle color changes and textures you'll see.
3. If you'd like to have garlic always on hand for a painting subject, set a few bulbs aside and let them dehydrate. They'll retain their shape and can be arranged and rearranged so they appear different in each painting.
4. When working on a medium to dark value background, let some of the background color show through the undercoat. This will help define the contours of the cloves, suggest texture, and unify the subject with the background. Apply the undercoat streakily, working from the base of the garlic to the tip.
5. Building up the opacity of the individual cloves at their fullest part (within the whole garlic) helps create dimension (see step 2).
6. Refer to all colors on lesson page to match and mix colors.

To create a faux woodgrained background, use a woodgraining comb or create a comb by cutting comb-like strips in a piece of heavy chipboard. Drag the comb through wet paint thinned with an extending medium (see page 49).

Try painting this bunch of hanging garlic using the pattern on the previous page.

2. Build up "bulges" with more Buttermilk, unthinned.

1. Use the flat brush to undercoat the garlic with thinned Buttermilk.

3. Apply a thin wash of Buttermilk over the entire garlic bulb.

4. Paint a streaky wash of Sand. Then undercoat the root area with Khaki Tan.

5. Sideload the flat brush with Khaki Tan to add shading.

6. Highlight the bulges with Light Buttermilk. Shade the roots and base with sideloaded Raw Umber.

Garlic Cloves

1. Undercoat individual cloves with Sand.

2. Paint a "streaky" wash of Khaki Tan, then accent with thinned French Mauve. Fill in the base end with Khaki Tan.

3. Sideload a flat brush with Black Plum + Raw Umber to add shading. Use the liner brush and Raw Umber + Black Plum to accent details.

7. Use the liner brush and thinned Light Buttermilk to paint the veins and broken skin details. Shade the details with thinned Raw Umber. Dab on Black Plum to accent.

8. Use the liner brush to paint the roots Sand + Khaki Tan. Highlight with Sand + Buttermilk. Add shadows in a thinned, darker value (Raw Umber + Black Plum) of background color (French Mauve).

Garlic Reference Photos

Growing your own garlic for painting subjects is really quite easy. In the fall, four to six weeks before the ground freezes, break open a garlic bulb, and plant the individual cloves about five inches apart and two inches deep in fertile soil and full sun. In the summer, when the leaves die back, pull the bulbs and dry them. Let a few of the more interesting shapes totally dry out. They'll make perfect painting models for years if handled gently.

LEMONS AND LIMES

While the worksheet is concerned primarily with painting lemons, it's easy to substitute colors to create the limes. The textured skins of citrus fruits, with their drybrushed highlights, add interesting contrast to a painting in which other fruits are all smooth skinned and shiny.

Limes

To paint limes, follow the process for painting the lemons but substitute the colors from the lime palette as follows:

- Undercoat the skins (including the edges of the cut slices) with Moon Yellow. Undercoat the rind with Buttermilk.
- Shade by dabbling Leaf Green (heavier where shading is to be darkest), then Avocado, letting some of the previous layers show through.
- Highlight by drybrushing with Titanium White.
- Sideload the brush with Moon Yellow and soften the edges where the yellow undercoat peeks through.
- To paint the flesh of the limes, follow the first three steps for lemon flesh. Then in step 4, apply a wash of Avocado over the flesh.

LEMONS PALETTE
- Cadmium Yellow
- Buttermilk
- Pineapple
- Light Avocado
- Tangerine
- Avocado
- Titanium White
- Orchid
- Moon Yellow

LIMES PALETTE
- Moon Yellow
- Buttermilk
- Leaf Green
- Avocado
- Titanium White

BRUSHES
- Flat: No. 8
- Round: No. 2
- Liner: No. 10/0

Hints

1. Use the flat brush to paint the skin, the flesh, and the leaves. Add details to the flesh with the liner brush. Paint the blossoms with the round brush (optional).

2. To create an interesting texture for the skin, tap or dab on your undercoat paint for lemons and limes, rather than merely brush it on. Use thick, undiluted paint, drying well between coats.

3. The texture of the skin can be emphasized by drybrushing on highlights. Be sure to wipe most of the paint off the brush onto a paper towel before attacking the fruit. The highlight color will "catch" on just the raised portions of the undercoat. You can continue adding layers until you achieve the effect you want, but it's hard to undo a too-heavy application (see Drybrushing, page 19).

4. Refer to all colors on the lesson page to match and mix colors.

The warmth of these bright, sunny colors is intensified by the hard, dark red cast shadow, showing us that the light casting is close and hot. Even the leaves are a warm green. Thank goodness for the cool relief of the blue-green lime.

Lime
(See instructions for painting limes on previous page.)

Lime Palette

(See instructions for painting limes on previous page.)

Border
(See illustration below.)

Create a border by painting repeated sections. To paint the flowers, load the round brush with Buttermilk, then dip the tip in Titanium White. Paint a pair of comma strokes for each petal. Use the liner to draw thin stamens of Cadmium Yellow. Add pollen dots of Pineapple.

Lemons, Leaves, and Flowers Palette

1. Dab two or three heavy coats of Cadmium Yellow on the whole lemon. Undercoat the cut lemon rind with Buttermilk. Use the round brush to stroke Pineapple on the flesh to form ridges. Undercoat the leaves with Light Avocado.

2. Dab the lower third of the whole lemon lightly with Tangerine, leaving a thin edge of undercoat showing along the bottom. Dab thinned Cadmium Yellow on the flesh of the slice. Outline the lower edge of the slice with Cadmium Yellow + Tangerine. Brush a thin layer of water on the leaves, then add a center vein and splotches with Avocado.

Lime Flesh

3. Dab or drybrush Titanium White on the upper part of the lemon. Use the liner to paint tiny straight comma strokes of Titanium White on the flesh of the slice. Brush a scant amount of water on the leaves, then add splotches of Light Avocado + Pineapple. Enhance shading on the whole lemon with a sideload of Orchid.

4. To merge the shading into the whole lemon, brush thinned Tangerine over it. Brush thinned Moon Yellow over the flesh and rind of the cut slice. Paint veins on the leaves with thinned Light Avocado + Pineapple. Then brush a thinned layer of Light Avocado over the leaves to blend colors softly. Add accent colors on the leaves, if desired, using any reds, purples, or deeper greens (see leaves in the border below).

Lemons and Limes Reference Photos

Lemons and limes are strong accents, both visually and intuitively—our lips can't help but pucker when we see them. Combine them with oranges in a basket and you've got an analogous color scheme of yellow, green, and orange.

MUSHROOMS

Even though mushrooms are not vegetables (they're fungi),
I've included them in this book because they've been
appreciated for their flavor since the time of the early
Greeks and Romans.

PALETTE
· Antique White
· Raw Sienna
· Dark Chocolate
· Midnite Blue
· Banana Cream

BRUSHES
· Flat: No. 8
· Liner: No. 10/0

Hints

1. Use the flat brush to paint the mushroom stems and caps, and the liner brush to paint the gills and tears.
2. Don't frustrate yourself by trying to copy these mushrooms exactly. You'll have more fun and greater success by just using the suggested steps and colors, and letting your random brush strokes guide where smudges, tears, dents, and wrinkles fall.
3. Buy a package of fresh mushrooms and dump them on a shelf near your painting area. Pick a few interesting ones to serve as models. You can even use the outline of the patterns provided and simply plug in details from your models.
4. Refer to all colors on the lesson page to match and mix colors.

Mushrooms, chili peppers, garlic, cherry tomatoes, and herbs.
See a photograph of these delectables on page 85.

1. Undercoat with Antique White.

2. Brush on a thin layer of water or water plus medium. Then immediately brush on thinned Raw Sienna, allowing it to appear splotchy.

3. Sideload the flat brush with Dark Chocolate + Midnite Blue. Fill in the gill area, placing the loaded side of the brush deep inside the cap and letting the color fade as it works up the base of the stem. Add dark smudges and creases by painting with the corner of the brush.

4. With the brush still sideloaded with Dark Chocolate + Midnite Blue, add shading to the cap and the stem. Add some color variations by shading in spots with just sideloaded Dark Chocolate.

5. Highlight with sideloaded Banana Cream. Then add a reflected light with very little Banana Cream + Raw Sienna.

6. Repeat any of the previous steps to adjust and/or strengthen hues and values. Add gills where appropriate with the liner and Raw Sienna. Paint cast shadows a darker value of the background color (in this case Dark Chocolate + Midnite Blue).

Mushrooms Reference Photos

Just look at all the wonderful smudges, scars, and irregularities on these mushrooms. They're not perfect. So relax when you paint them; don't blend their subtle colors to oblivion! After trying the mushrooms in the lesson, have some fun painting uniquely shaped and colored wild mushrooms. You might even create your own fanciful fungi.

Onions

The word "onion" comes from the Latin *unio*, which means large pearl. In this lesson, we'll paint three large pearls, each a different color.

RED ONIONS PALETTE
- Napa Red
- Moon Yellow
- Deep Burgundy
- Burnt Umber

WHITE ONIONS PALETTE
- Eggshell
- Buttermilk
- Light Buttermilk
- Jade Green
- Neutral Grey
- Titanium White

YELLOW ONIONS PALETTE
- Moon Yellow
- Buttermilk
- Terra Cotta
- Burnt Orange
- Cadmium Yellow
- Burnt Umber
- Raw Umber

BRUSHES
- Flats: Nos. 2 and 8
- Liner: No. 10/0

Hints

1. Use the No. 8 flat brush to paint the onion, the No. 2 flat brush to paint detailed areas of broken skin, and the liner brush to paint the roots.

2. If you're working on a dark background, you can omit step 1 and let the dark background show through step 2 to suggest the vein lines in the onion skin. Pay attention to the contour lines (see sidebar at right).

3. If the highlight seems too strong when you first apply it in step 2, don't worry. Subsequent layers of thinned washes will be applied over it to submerge it "into" the onion. Try to keep the wash layers thin, though, so you don't lose the light/dark variations that suggest the vein-like texture in the onion skin. If you should lose the veins, paint them back in with the liner, using very thinned paint to keep them from appearing too overworked.

4. The instructions on the following page are for red onions. Change the colors as described below to paint the white and yellow onions.
   - **White onions**: Use Eggshell to undercoat, Buttermilk to contour and highlight, Light Buttermilk to apply the first wash, Jade Green and Neutral Grey to paint the flesh under the broken skin and to shade and create additional wash color variations, and Titanium White to add final wash adjustments and highlights.
   - **Yellow onions**: Use Moon Yellow to undercoat, Buttermilk to contour and highlight, Terra Cotta to paint outer layers of skin, Burnt Umber to wash a reddish glow onto the skin, Terra Cotta to apply shading to the exposed flesh, Cadmium Yellow as a wash for creating color variations, Burnt Umber for shading, and Raw Umber then Moon Yellow for the roots.

5. Refer to all colors on the lesson page to match and mix colors.

Contour Lines

Notice how the contour lines radiate out from the bold center line. Letting your brush strokes follow these lines will help establish the roundness of the subject.

1. Undercoat with Napa Red, working from base to tip and following the contours of the onion.

2. Streak from base to tip with Moon Yellow sideloaded on the flat brush and continue to highlight with Moon Yellow.

3. (a) Cover the onion with a wash of Napa Red. Dry thoroughly. (b) Apply a slightly heavier wash of Deep Burgundy.

4. Sideload the brush with Napa Red and paint the broken skin area. Use thinner paint in the highlight area and heavier paint near the base and along the edges of the broken skin.

5. Brush very thin Moon Yellow across the inside skin area to reestablish the highlight and on some edges of the broken skin.

6. Add roots by painting a sideloaded smudge of Burnt Umber at the base; use the liner to paint fine roots with Burnt Umber + Moon Yellow.

Red Onions Palette

White Onions Palette

Yellow Onions Palette

Onions Reference Photos

Use a paper punch to make a hole in white paper. Hold it at arm's length and, closing one eye, look at the onion through the hole with the other eye. By isolating the colors like this, you'll be able to see more clearly how much color is actually reflected. Notice, also, how the vein lines mark the contours of the onions.

ORANGES

Review the hints for painting lemons and limes (page 78).
Using thick enough paint to create a dimpled texture in the
orange skin will help suggest realism.

PALETTE
- Cadmium Yellow
- Tangerine
- Burnt Orange
- Blue Violet
- Titanium White
- Light Avocado

BRUSHES
- Flat: No. 8
- Round: No. 2

Hints

1. Review the hints for painting
   lemons and limes on page 78.
   Using thick enough paint to create
   a dimpled texture in the orange
   skin will help suggest realism.
2. Use the flat brush to paint the
   orange skin and flesh and the
   round brush to paint details on
   the flesh.
3. Make the orange slightly irregular
   in shape, not perfectly round.
4. Imagine painting this orange
   on a blue background. If you
   apply the orange color thinly on
   the part of the fruit in shadow,
   some of the blue background
   would show through. Our eyes
   would mix the orange and the
   blue visually, creating a lovely,
   appropriate shading color. When
   the background is a dark color, or
   particularly a dark complementary
   color, letting some of it shine
   through the undercoat of the
   object helps model the object or
   shade it.
5. Refer to all colors on the lesson
   page to match and mix colors.

The marbleized texture of this background repeats
somewhat the texture of the flesh of the orange in this
monochromatic color scheme.

In this complementary scheme, the textured
background tugs the gaze away from the orange
—unlike the lack of competition from the
solid red background.

In this analogous scheme, the orange stands out as a
bright beacon against the solid red background, which
offers no textural competition.

Here the combination of the orange with the blue-
green and blue-violet background results in a split
complementary color scheme.

1. Undercoat the orange with Cadmium Yellow, tapping the paint on thickly to suggest texture.

2. Apply a thin, splotchy wash of Tangerine, letting more light value undercoat show in the upper right highlight areas.

3. Load the brush with an extender medium, then sideload with a mixture of Tangerine + Burnt Orange plus very little Blue Violet and shade the left side.

4. Load the flat brush with scant Cadmium Yellow plus a little Titanium White, and wipe nearly dry. Hold the brush parallel to the painting and lightly skim across the top third to highlight. Shade around the stem depression and paint the creases with Tangerine + Burnt Orange + Blue Violet.

5. Accent the highlight, using more Titanium White and less Cadmium Yellow, applying the paint in the center of the highlight area. Paint the stem and calyx Light Avocado + Cadmium Yellow + Titanium White.

6. Sideload the flat brush with Cadmium Yellow + Titanium White and paint a stroke of reflected light along the lower left edge of the orange. Highlight the stem with Cadmium Yellow + Titanium White + Light Avocado; shade it with Light Avocado + Burnt Orange + Blue Violet. Paint a wash of Cadmium Yellow over the stem.

Slice

1. (a) Dab on Cadmium Yellow thickly to create textured flesh. (b) Dab on a splotchy wash of Cadmium Yellow + Tangerine plus very little Blue Violet. (c) Paint the membrane next to the rind using Titanium White + Cadmium Yellow + Tangerine. Paint the rind as described above.

2. Use the round brush to paint the white membrane at the center of the slice with Titanium White + Cadmium Yellow + Tangerine. Without rinsing the brush, dip it in extender and roll it on the flesh to create irregular lines.

3. Apply a wash of Cadmium Yellow + Burnt Orange over the flesh, membrane, and rind. Add a shadow in the membrane at the top of the slice and under the orange with Blue Violet + Burnt Orange + Titanium White.

Oranges Reference Photos

Oranges look so appealing and have such delightful patterns when they're sliced. Orange peels with their hand-torn edges and random shapes add a delightful contrast to a composition. The orange on the weathered boards casts a hard shadow from the brilliant sunlight. And look at how the color of the orange deepens into red as it gets farther away from the light.

PEACHES

The characteristic peach fuzz is accomplished by painting a thin overlay of light color on the nearly completed fruit. Be sure to let some of the fuzz extend slightly beyond the edges of the peach.

PALETTE
- Moon Yellow
- Terra Coral
- Naphthol Red
- Peaches 'n Cream
- Light Avocado
- Olive Green
- Midnite Green
- Peacock Teal
- Shale Green

BRUSHES
- Flats: Nos. 4 and 8
- Round: No. 2
- Liner: No. 10/0
- Round fabric (Series FAB): No. 4

Hints

1. Use the No. 8 flat brush to paint the peach and leaves, the No. 4 flat brush to shade the stem depression, and the round brush to paint the stem. Use the liner brush to paint details on the leaves, and the fabric brush with its stiff bristles to add texture to the peach.

2. When you undercoat the peach, use thick paint and tap or stipple the last coat to create texture and to suggest velvety skin.

3. Refer to all colors on the lesson page to match and mix colors.

I used a soft pastel background here to echo the velvet softness of the peach skin. Notice how much more interesting the gradated background is than if it had been a solid color.

Leaves

To paint the leaves (see the illustrations below), follow this process, substituting different greens for variety.

· (a) Undercoat with Shale Green, then (b) apply a puddly wash of Light Avocado, Olive Green, Midnite Green, or Peacock Teal.
· Sideload the No. 4 flat brush with Midnite Green. Paint along the center vein and dab on shading sporadically.
· Sideload the No. 4 flat brush with Terra Coral to accent, then with Moon Yellow to highlight.
· Use the liner brush to paint veins with Olive Green and to paint "bug-eaten" parts with the stem mixture, Terra Coral + Light Avocado.

1. Undercoat the peach with two or three coats of Moon Yellow (see hint 2). Undercoat the stem using the round brush and Terra Coral + Light Avocado.

2. Brush a coat of extender medium on the peach. Use the fabric brush to pounce on Terra Coral, heavily in some areas and lightly in others. Highlight the stem using the stem mixture plus Moon Yellow.

3. Sideload the flat brush with Naphthol Red to shade the cleft and deepen the peach's blush. Shade the stem with the stem mixture plus Midnite Green.

4. Sideload the flat brush with Peaches 'n Cream and highlight the front edge of the cleft. Dry completely. Then lightly brush sideloaded Peaches 'n Cream over the entire peach, using the clear side of the brush to "tickle" the color gently over areas where less is desired.

5. Sideload the flat brush with Light Avocado and shade the stem depression.

Leaves
(See instructions above.)

Peaches Reference Photos

It's easy to identify peach trees in the orchard (during non-fruiting periods that is) by their long, slender leaves. Using the photos, compare the bark with that of other fruit trees. Notice how closely the peach is attached to the branch. Its stem is but a stub.

Pomegranates

A fond childhood memory is my first encounter with this curious fruit and its juicy, pulp-covered seeds. Giving our own children a pomegranate became a fun, fall family tradition, continued even after they were grown. We've extended the tradition, now, to include our grandchildren. A cut pomegranate offers lots of interesting detail for a painting.

PALETTE
- Flesh Tone
- Sand
- Berry Red
- Antique White
- Cranberry Wine
- Raw Umber
- Spice Pink
- Cadmium Red
- Tangerine

BRUSHES
- Flats: Nos. 2, 6, and 10
- Round: No. 2
- Liner: No. 10/0

Hints

1. Use the No. 10 flat brush to apply undercoats and all washes. Use the No. 6 flat brush to detail the flesh in step 2, and the No. 2 flat brush to paint the seeds in step 3. Use the round brush to highlight the seeds, and the liner brush to fill in the blossom end and paint the pollen.
2. Don't bother tracing the seeds. It's much easier to paint them freehand. Use the No. 2 flat brush, forming two crescent strokes for each seed.
3. Notice on the worksheet how the spilled juice makes the area it covers appear darker.
4. Refer to all colors on the lesson page to match and mix colors.

1. Undercoat the skin with Flesh Tone. Undercoat the flesh with Sand.

2. Apply a wash of Berry Red to the skin. Dab Antique White on the flesh.

3. Apply a wash of Cranberry Wine to the skin, heavier on the right and base. Paint the seeds with careless crescent-shaped strokes of sideloaded Cranberry Wine.

4. With the liner brush, fill in the blossom end with lines of Raw Umber. Use the round brush to highlight seeds with Spice Pink, then dot with Spice Pink + Sand.

5. Apply a wash of Berry Red over most of the flesh. Dry. Apply a wash of Cadmium Red randomly over the flesh. Paint the pollen and highlight the blossom end with Flesh Tone.

6. Drybrush the skin with Flesh Tone. Apply a wash of Tangerine over the flesh area, keeping it thin on the whitish membrane.

7. Add a blemish or two with thinned Raw Umber, outlined with Flesh Tone.

8. Paint the spilled juice with Cadmium Red + Berry Red. Highlight the juice with Sand.

Pomegranates Reference Photos

Pomegranates look like they have already started to explode, even before they are cut open. That's why it is such fun to paint them opened up with juices dribbling all over. Their almost coarse-textured skin is interesting to paint, as well.

STRAWBERRIES

We converted the front yard at our old mill home to an herb garden and strawberry patch. I have to race to the patch each morning to gather berries for our cereal before the chipmunks carry them off to sit on the rock wall fence and sample the free fare.

PALETTE

- Peaches 'n Cream
- Coral Blush
- Cadmium Red
- Cranberry Wine
- Moon Yellow
- Banana Cream
- Light Avocado
- Spa Blue
- Black Forest Green
- Yellow Green

BRUSHES

- Flats: Nos. 2 and 8
- Round: No. 0
- Liner: No. 10/0

Hints

1. Use the No. 8 flat brush to paint the berries and leaves, the No. 2 flat brush to paint the calyxes, the round brush to paint the seed depressions and the seeds, and the liner to paint highlights around the seed depressions.
2. Suggested painting sequence: Paint the entire berry first, then the seeds, then the calyx.
3. Note in step 2 the heavier application of the wash color on the left (shadow) side of the berry.
4. To highlight the berry in step 4, use a sideloaded brush, keeping the paint edge of the brush toward the center of the highlight. Use the water edge of the brush to blend and soften the edges of the highlight.
5. Seed depressions: Stagger their placement so they don't line up like tin soldiers. Highlight all the way around a few in the center of the strong highlight area. Highlight on the left of those to the left of the highlight and on the right of those to the right of the highlight. (Remember how the light affected the depression in the ball of clay in exercise 2, page 37.)
6. Refer to all colors on the lesson page to match and mix colors.

Notice how I repeated the red of the berries in the leaves.

1. **Berry:** Undercoat with Peaches 'n Cream. **Calyx:** Undercoat with Light Avocado, heavier in some places.

2. **Berry:** Float a wash of Coral Blush over the entire berry. **Calyx:** Shade with a mixture of Light Avocado + Cranberry Wine.

3. **Berry:** Shade the berry with Cranberry Wine. **Calyx:** Highlight with Banana Cream.

4. **Berry:** Highlight with Banana Cream.

5. **Berry:** Form the seed depressions on the berry with a thinned mixture of Cadmium Red + Cranberry Wine. **Calyx:** Tint with washes of Moon Yellow.

6. **Berry:** Highlight around the seed depressions on the berry with Banana Cream, noting both the position and amount of highlight on the illustration. **Seeds:** Paint with Moon Yellow. **Calyx:** Tint with washes of Coral Blush.

7. **Berry:** Cover with a wash of Cadmium Red. While it is damp, lift color off of the highlight area. Then, add a reflected light using a mixture of Spa Blue + Banana Cream. Add cast shadows with a mixture of Cranberry Wine + Light Avocado. **Calyx:** Strengthen the light and dark values if needed.

Leaves

1. Undercoat with Light Avocado.

2. Paint veins with Black Forest Green.

3. Cover with a puddly wash of Black Forest Green.

4. (a) Highlight with Yellow Green + Moon Yellow. (b) Shade with Black Forest Green. (c) Add tints with Cadmium Red and with Black Forest Green.

Strawberries Reference Photos

Look closely at the blossoms to see strawberries beginning to form within them. Note the shape and margins of the three-part leaves. Locate the strongest, broadest highlight area on the single strawberry. It's to the right of the center axis. Now look at the stem depressions to the right of that highlight. Where are the highlights on them? Then look at the depressions to the far left of that center axis. Where are the highlights on those depressions?

TOMATOES

The tomato is really a fruit because the edible portion contains the seeds; vegetables consist of edible stems, roots, and leaves. Fruit or vegetable, the tomato is a wonderful subject to paint.

PALETTE
- Yellow Ochre
- Cadmium Red
- Tomato Red
- Deep Burgundy
- Desert Turquoise
- Avocado
- Black Green
- Antique Gold

BRUSHES
- Flat: No. 12
- Round: No. 4

Hints

1. Use the flat brush to paint the tomato and the round brush to paint the calyx.
2. In painting this tomato we will let the highlight area shine from within, rather than applying light value paint on top of our paint layers. To do this, first apply a thin, even layer of water plus extender medium. Remove any excess water so the surface is just barely, but evenly, damp. Then, beginning at the edge of the tomato, and working with a large, sideloaded brush, apply a red wash up to and just over the edge of the highlight area. The red paint will disperse gradually into the damp area, leaving a softened edge. Avoid the tendency to overwork this step. The paint will soon start to "grab." Let it dry. Repeat the step as needed to get the depth of color desired. If the wash covers too much of the highlight area, blot immediately with a damp brush to lift out the excess color.
3. Some tomatoes have creases at the stem end. If you would like to add them, sideload the flat brush with a red that is slightly darker than the area on which you will be painting the crease. Apply the paint along one side of the crease line then immediately flip the brush to apply the sideloaded paint to the other side of the crease. Blend to remove any hard-edged paint lines in the crease (see Edge-to-Edge Blending on page 20).
4. In painting the calyx, add shading and highlighting by applying thinned paint in fine streaks, following the growth direction from base to tip.
5. Refer to all colors on the lesson page to match and mix colors.

Compare this warm/cool color scheme with the warm/cool one on the worksheet.

Calyx

1. Undercoat with Avocado.

2. Shade with Avocado + Black Green. Highlight with Yellow Ochre + Avocado.

3. Apply a wash of Antique Gold + Avocado.

6. Add a reflected light by sideloading the flat brush with Desert Turquoise plus very little Yellow Ochre. Shade indentations with a sideload of Cadmium Red + Tomato Red, or on darker tomatoes with Deep Burgundy.

Tomato

1. Undercoat the tomato with Yellow Ochre.

2. Apply a thin wash of Cadmium Red. Dry completely.

3. Apply a thin layer of extender medium to the highlight area. While it is wet, apply another wash of Cadmium Red, working it gently onto the edges of the damp area. Allow to dry. Repeat the step until you're satisfied with the depth of color achieved.

4. Apply a wash of Tomato Red as in step 3.

5. Shade with a wash of Deep Burgundy, again leaving the highlight area light.

Tomatoes Reference Photos

Learning to adapt and change reference material to suit your needs multiplies your opportunities to explore, learn, and make effective substitutions.

GLOSSARY

A

Accent: A small application of color to add interest, such as a blush of red on a pear, or a tinge of brown on a leaf.

Acetate: A lightweight, plastic-like transparent sheet; useful for testing colors, strokes, and designs before placing them on a project.

Analogous: Describes a color scheme that includes any two to seven adjacent colors on the color wheel (for example: yellow, blue, and green).

B

Background color: The underlying color of a painted piece.

Basecoat: The initial coat(s) of paint applied to an item to prepare it for additional layers of colors and design work; the background color.

Bright: A type of flat brush with short hairs; sometimes called a chisel brush. Also describes color that is clear, brilliant, and intense.

Bristles: The hairs of a brush; more specifically, the stiffer types of hair such as hog or boar bristles.

Brush blending: Mixing two or more colors together by picking up a little of each with a brush, rather than a palette knife, and stroking, not stirring, them together on the palette.

C

Calyx: The group of leaf-like sepals at the stem end of a flower or fruit.

Cast shadow: A shadow caused by an object blocking the flow of light.

Chalk pencil: A pencil with chalk in place of graphite; used in designing. Chalk can be easily removed with a damp cloth.

Chisel edge: The bottom edge of a flat brush.

Complementary colors: Colors that are located diametrically opposite one another on the color wheel (for example, red and green). They neutralize one another when mixed.

Contour lines: Lines that indicate the dimensional form of an object.

Cool colors: Colors that appear to recede or move away from the viewer (greens, blues, violets).

Cured: Pertaining to the state at which paint, after being applied, has thoroughly hardened through the completion of all internal drying and chemical processes.

D

Doubleloading: The process of loading two colors or values of paint onto one brush so that each color retains its identity while at the same time creating a mixture of the two colors in the center of the brush.

Drybrushing: A technique of applying paint using a brush with very little paint.

E

Extender: A type of painting medium, that, when added to acrylic paints, prolongs the drying time.

F

Faux finish: Fake finish; technique of painting something to look like something else (for example, painting wood to resemble marble).

Ferrule: The metal cylinder in which the hairs of a brush are glued and the handle firmly fastened.

Flat brush: A brush having hairs that taper to a flat chisel edge.

Floated color: A thin layer of color that is stroked onto a film of water or painting medium over a dry undercoat color.

Focal area: The center of interest in a painting.

Fully loaded: Describes a brush that is thoroughly filled with a single color of paint.

G

Gradated: Describes an application of paint that progresses from strong to faded color. This effect is usually achieved with a sideloaded brush.

H

Hairs: The bristles of a brush.

Highlight: A representation of the bright reflection of a direct light source.

Hue: Another word for color.

I

Intensity: The pureness or saturation of a color.

Intermediary colors: Colors that lie in between the primary and secondary colors on the color wheel (for example, red-orange, yellow-green, and blue-violet). They are created by mixing a primary color with a neighboring secondary color.

L

Light source: The primary source of illumination of an object; determines position of highlighting and shading.

Liner brush: A brush with a round ferrule housing a small amount of bristles to achieve a fine line when used with paints, inks, and watercolors. The hairs range from short to long.

Local color: The dominant color of an object.

M

Marbleizing: A faux finish technique in which paint is applied to resemble marble.

Medium: A product that is added to paint to prolong the drying time and to render the paint more flexible and easier to work with.

Monochromatic: Describes a color scheme that includes tints and shades of a single hue (for example, light and dark blues).

P

Palette knife: An artist's implement used to mix and apply paint.

Pigment: Material (such as finely ground powder) that adds color to paint.

Primary colors: Red, blue, and yellow; these three colors are necessary for mixing all other colors in the color spectrum.

R

Reflected light: Illumination that is reflected off of an object rather than coming directly from the light source.

Round brush: A brush with hairs formed into a cylinder and tapering to a point.

S

Scumbling: A technique that involves the loose application of color in unconnected strokes to create a broken-color effect.

Secondary colors: Orange, green, and violet; each secondary color is created by mixing together two primary colors.

Sepal: One of a cluster of small leaves comprising the calyx at the base of a flower or fruit.

Shading: A slight variation or difference of color to have a shadowing effect on the area opposite of a light produced area. This is achieved by adding a darker pigmentation or black paint to the main color.

Sideloading: The loading of paint onto only one side or edge of a brush.

Split-complementary: Describes a color scheme that consists of three colors: a main color and the two colors on either side of the main color's complement (for example, yellow, red-violet, and blue-violet).

Sponging: A faux finish technique of applying paint with a sponge to achieve a mottled effect.

Stippling: A method of applying paint to achieve a speckled color effect by repeatedly dabbing with the brush.

Stylized: Describes a design characterized by simplification of form.

Stylus: An implement with a small, rounded point used in transferring designs and to create paint dots. A good substitute is a "dead" ballpoint pen.

T

Taklon: A synthetic filament used as hairs in some brushes.

Temperature: The perceived warmth or coolness of a color. Warm colors advance; cool colors recede.

Tertiary colors: Colors that result from the mixture of two secondary colors. Each tertiary color contains all three primary colors.

Tint: Color that is created by adding a lighter value or white to any color.

Tone: Color that is created by adding black plus white to any color.

Transfer: To copy a pattern either freehand or by use of a specially treated artist's transfer paper.

Transfer paper: A paper coated with chalk, graphite, or other substance that, when placed between the pattern and the object to be decorated, aids in the transferring of the design.

Triadic: Describes a color scheme that includes any three colors equidistant from one another on the color wheel (for example, red, yellow, and blue).

U

Undercoat: The first layer of color used to define the shape and basic color of the subject matter, to be followed by highlighting and shading colors.

V

Value: A color's relation to white or black or the grays in between; the lightness or darkness of a color.

Value scale: A scale that specifies nine distinct steps of gray between black and white; created by Henry Albert Munsell, an early American portrait painter.

W

Warm colors: Colors that appear to advance or move toward the viewer (reds, oranges, yellows).

Wash: A layer of thin paint applied over a dry layer of paint to alter its color slightly.

INDEX

Note: Page numbers in *italics* indicate step-by-step lessons.